Crack the Spine
XVII

Edited by Kerri Farrell Foley

Collection Copyright © 2018 Crack the Spine

ISBN 978-0-9889782-9-4

Individual works are the sole property of the authors.

Published by Crack the Spine Literary Magazine
Printed in the United States of America

Crack the Spine Literary Magazine
Houston, Texas ~ Galveston, Texas
www.crackthespine.com

Table of Contents

Robert Fillman

Commercial for a Midlife Crisis

The vanishing glow
of December sunset
through a bay window

betrays a daughter,
her wet moon smile,

breast bones exposed
like sweating basement pipes

no longer concealed
by sheer rose-print.

She slides backward, feels
the shriveled yank
of an incision,

embarrassment
at the thought

of her own mother,

eyebrows like cleavers,

changing

brown, bloody gauze,

over and over

the way she reassured

men would still love her

like so many

paper hearts.

Robert Fillman has been a finalist for the Gerald Cable Book Award. His poems have
appeared or are forthcoming in *The Hollins Critic, Poet Lore, Poetry East, Salamander, Tar
River Poetry,* and others. Fillman's poem 'Dumping Leaves' was a winner
in *Thira Wednesday*'s 2017 annual poetry contest, and in 2016 he won first prize in
poetry at the Pennsylvania Writers Conference. A Ph.D. candidate and Senior
Teaching Fellow at Lehigh University, he lives in eastern Pennsylvania with his wife,
Melissa, and their two children, Emma and Robbie.

Crickets

"Did you see the guy selling huge stick bugs?" I say to Mike as I approach our table. I push a dolly stacked with Rubbermaid containers into our booth space. Mike must've just gotten here because he's unloading, too.

"No dude, but is that all he's got? It's not Insect Swap."

"I mean, true, but at the same time, people can sell anything that appeals to the reptile crowd. I just saw a t-shirt table. And there are always insects—crickets."

"Crickets are just food," Mike says. "And that table is probably lame t-shirts with reptiles on them."

I look down at my own shirt. It's black and reads "Geckō Unlimited" under an Eckō Unltd. logo modified to look like a gecko. I bought it months ago but saved it for today.

"Crickets are cool, too," I say. Before I got into reptiles I liked insects. "You've probably only seen the two kinds usually used for feeding. There are ones with stripes and stuff. And different kinds sing different songs."

Mike carefully pulls a tall vivarium out of a huge cardboard box and sets it on his side of the table.

"Are those leaf-tailed geckos?" I rush over and put my face so close to the glass that my breath fogs it up and I have to back away. The geckos are long and blend in with the dried leaves also in the tank. "You didn't mention these in the forums."

Before Mike can answer me, he's fielding questions from potential customers. The event staff must've opened the doors early. I hurry to set up my four small tanks of day geckos, one color per tank—green, yellow, blue, and green with red spots.

We spend the morning talking to customers. The stream of people is large enough that we can mostly avoid talking to each other. Even though my geckos are brighter in color, many people are selling day geckos, so passers-by are more enthralled by Mike's leaf-taileds.

After a few hours, Mike covers up his vivarium with its cardboard box. "I'm going to go walk around and see what's out there," he says. "You don't mind, right buddy?"

"Not at all," I say, though I don't know why he wouldn't just ask me to handle his business. He's sold all of the geckos he brought in except for two, which he wants to keep to show people, and is now just taking down email addresses of interested buyers. I've only sold one day gecko so far. I'd rather take down email addresses for Mike than have to tell people the leaf-tailed guy will be back shortly.

After Mike walks off, I notice the cardboard box is too large for his tank. It hangs, angled, off the back of the table. Just a small nudge would probably bring the whole tank crashing to the floor. The tank probably cost Mike hundreds of dollars. I'd be really upset if any of my tanks broke, and they're less than half the size. I stay seated on my side of the table and look at my day geckos. Their colors are so bright. Why wouldn't that be popular? I guess even the bright colors are easy to get. People are more impressed by rare things these days, even if they're uglier.

Mike returns with a clear, plastic container in his hand. He holds it up, smirking. It contains a brown stick bug.

"What?" I say, because I can't think of anything better.

"Don't be jealous," Mike says, laughing, "But it was his last one."

"I wasn't going to buy a stick bug anyway," I say. With my lack of sales, I'll probably lose money on the Reptile Swap this year. Can't go around buying things and making my loss even bigger.

"That's right," Mike says. "You like crickets. Well, you're in luck! I can give you a whole bag!" He pulls a bag of at least fifty crickets from one of his boxes and holds it out toward me.

I reach out with both hands and rip the bag open.

"Hey!" Mike says. I stare in his eyes and do not look away. Crickets jump out of the bag onto his hands, his arms, our table, the floor. I feel one land on the top of my head, but I keep looking at Mike.

"It was just a joke, man," he says.

"I know," I say. "That's also why I ripped the bag. For a joke."

Mike opens his mouth to say something else, but a cricket jumps into it. I laugh as he drops the bag then coughs and spits cricket onto the floor. He looks at me as if he wants me to help. I shrug. Mike sticks his tongue out and scrapes at it frantically with his fingers. A few people walking by stop, trying to figure out what he's doing.

"He almost ate a cricket!" I say. "Isn't that hilarious?" I laugh and the people walking laugh, and I laugh some more.

"It sure looks like it tasted bad!" I say, but the people who were laughing have already walked on to the next table.

Jay Vera Summer is a writer and artist living in Florida. She loves animals, plants, and water. Her work may be found in *marieclaire.com, Proximity, Luna Luna Magazine,* and more. She cofounded the online literary magazine *weirderary.*

Jamie Elliot Keith

The Deal

North Alabama, 1969

Wilbur Sands rubbed his hands together and would have heard the dry rasp of hard-worn farmer's hands if he'd been listening. His ears were as keen as when he was a boy tracking squirrels for dinner, but he had his mind on the load of firewood he'd just piled into the back of his Ford pickup. He slammed the tailgate, in a hurry to get going. His knuckles, knotted like the kindling he'd piled on top of the split logs, ached from the damp and the skin on his forefingers was cracked. He'd have to start with the Corn Huskers lotion again despite that fruity smell.

Last week he'd struck a deal with Abner Reaves, known to everyone who knew him as Abby. He'd deliver a load of wood to Abby's house up to Hamilton this afternoon in exchange for some replacement gears and new seals Wilbur needed to tune up his tractor for spring planting. The catch being Abby planned to get the parts off his brother-in-law. Having dealt with Abby in the past, Wilbur suffered some serious doubts about whether this deal would actually come to be. Abby, a cagey little man who combed his thin hair back straight from his forehead—slicked it down with Brylcreem or some other goo—had practice at shirking his side of the bargain. Then, again, when you'd least expect it he'd come through.

Wilbur didn't have much of choice. He needed the parts and he couldn't show his face around the hardware store with his long running account in arrears again. Earl hassled him the last few times he'd gone in. Earl's daddy lived his entire life as a farmer, as had half the Padgett Brothers customers, so you'd think he'd cut Wilbur some slack. Wilbur blamed all that new construction business. Padgett Brothers used to carry their long-time customers when they got in a pinch. Now they could turn their backs on the people who'd kept them in business all these years.

Though they'd called for it to rain the entire day, there'd been a break in early afternoon, so he'd loaded the wood in a sparse drizzle. About five minutes ago the branches had begun to thrash, pocking hickory nuts against the ancient toolshed's rusted roof. He raised his eyes to the low sky as a mass of dark clouds barreled in, a rerun of this morning. And sure enough, heavy raindrops began to spatter like scattershot. Time to get on the road.

Soon Wilbur was on the paved county by-way, and though it still poured, he could see better than down between the socked-in ridges where his house sat. He hated to think he had to unload all this wood in the drenching rain. Someone else might offer to help unload the truck, but no way would Abby lend a hand and pass up a chance to treat Wilbur like hired help. Wilbur could already see him warm and dry inside the old two-story house, with its fallen-down porch, peering out as Wilbur got soaked to the skin. Wilbur regretted he hadn't checked around more to find someone else willing to barter. Maybe Jeff Barnes or Charlie Proctor. Too late now for that now.

Wilbur reached into his shirt pocket and slipped out a crumpled pack of Lucky Strikes. Almost empty. He'd have to stop at the 7-Eleven on the way back; they'd be open on Sunday. He tapped the pack against his leg. A couple of cigarettes slid forward, and he wiggled one out with his lips. At least the cigarette lighter still worked. He slipped the pack back into his shirt pocket, pressed the glowing lighter against the end of the cigarette, and took a long pull. Okay. Might as well relax between here and Hamilton. It would be a slow trip with the rain. Besides, he planned on taking it easy to conserve gas. His wallet held a single ten-dollar bill and he hated to stop for only a few gallons. Made it look like he couldn't afford a whole tank. Which he couldn't.

He cracked the window and took another long draw. Not such a good idea to open the window in rain like this, but it was force of habit. Rosy gone now for four years and still he cracked the window. She didn't like him to smoke. Said it would kill him one day, and then she was the one to up and die. Four years.

A low groan like the dying note of bass fiddle rose from his gut. His Rosy. Sometimes it made him grind his teeth in anger. All those years in the last row of church, listening to Brother Vickers rant, standing to hum along with the hymns, closing his eyes in prayer, and sometimes even believing there might be someone out there listening. What had it bought him? Days like today, the dark skies, the soggy feel to everything. It made him sorry for himself.

Not a healthy thing. A man in his prime without a woman. He knew how to take care of things, but when he got done he felt dirty, like someone was watching. Surely Rosy would avert her eyes if she ever happened to be looking down on him. She understood the needs of a man. Wilbur felt a stirring and switched on the radio to get his mind on something else. Mostly static, so he kept fiddling with the tuning knob. Finally, he turned the volume off with a sharp twist. No matter. Even if you caught a station, half the time the radio shorted out. He'd get down under the dash and check the wires one of these days, but the only time he thought of it, he was behind the wheel.

He headed south to catch Highway 78. Even though Hamilton lay northwest of his place, he'd get there quicker on the state highway to 171 and then a straight shot north to Hamilton. Abby and his wife Dell lived on the far side of town. Less than ten minutes and he steered the truck west along the smooth asphalt of Highway 78. The tires slogged through the standing water. Only now and then did a spray of water from an oncoming vehicle splash across his windshield; there seemed to be more traffic traveling east than Wilbur's way.

As he slowed the truck to keep from skidding along the slick road, Wilbur saw a new model sedan pulled to the right shoulder, hunkered down in the rain, dark and empty. Ran out of gas he guessed. Bad luck on a day like today. He pumped the brake. He was relieved not to see anyone hitching a ride. A good Christian would stop, despite his wanting to get home to watch at least part of the Jets football game. Wilbur never liked to pull for a yankee team, but Joe Namath, a University of Alabama boy, played for Bear Bryant, quarterbacked the team to the Orange Bowl, and Wilbur'd followed him ever since.

Wilbur kept an eye on the side of the road and wondered who'd abandon a sharp-looking car like that. Could be a woman. He didn't know about that. If it was Rosie out here alone or his daughter Darlene he'd want someone to stop. Maybe. Hard to tell about who might do the stopping. He thought about it some more. It might be best to drive on by, act like he didn't see anyone. No temptations then.

He'd vowed to Rosie she'd always be the only one. And he stuck to it. Except the one time. He'd gone up towards Muscle Shoals to visit his mother's cousins and there was that girl. Fresh as a dew-kissed plum. She seemed kind of simple, not retarded—he wouldn't touch a retarded girl—but not all there. She acted like she wanted it. Only that one time; well, two if you counted the time he'd just turned fourteen. It was just touching, and the little girl was too young to remember anything anyway. Besides, he hadn't met Rosie yet, so it didn't really count.

There, on up ahead. He saw two forms crowded under a small umbrella. Women best he could tell; no man would fool with an umbrella on a day like today. Two women. A pity to pass them by in this downpour. He slowed alongside, the right wheels, front and back, crunching on the gravelly shoulder.

Wilbur leaned over and rolled down the passenger window. "Need a ride?"

The two women looked at each other. One was tall, a big woman. The other, small and pale with dark eyes and hair.

"I'm Wilbur Sands from over by Brilliant." Wilbur saw the blank glance pass between them. "I'm headed to Hamilton."

"We ran out of gas," the big gal said.

"Well, get on in. Hamilton's probably the closest." The two women climbed in, the big redhead next to him and the other woman, with dainty features and a timid way about her, near the window. She reminded him a little bit of a citified Rosie.

"You two young ladies look like drowned rats." Wilbur laughed. Definitely not farm women. He noted the soaked raincoats, the stained high heels on the smaller woman. Dressed up, out in the rain. "I'll bet you clean up pretty nice. What in the world were you thinking driving out alone in a gully-washer like this?"

"Trying to get home to Tupelo," the tall red-head said. Wilbur wagered she wouldn't put up with much from anybody. Still, he was the one with the truck.

"Y'all got husbands? Somebody gonna be worried about you?" Wilbur reached for his half-smoked cigarette perched in the ashtray. "Don't mind the smoke, do you?" He took a drag. Not too smart these two, out in weather like this, accepting a ride from some unknown man.

"We sure appreciate the ride." The big one laughed. "I'm Charlene. Charlene Farris. And this is Evvie Carroll."

"I don't know if I'd like my girls taking a ride from a stranger. Couldn't see driving by without checking on y'all, though." He caught a whiff of flowers. Perfume. He wondered if they could smell the dried sweat on him, lathered up when he'd loaded all that wood.

"We sure appreciate it." Charlene laughed again. "That one little umbrella wasn't doing us much good."

"It's a far walk to a gas station from out here. 'Specially in them fancy shoes." Wilbur nodded his head toward the far floorboard. The small one, Evvie, had torn her nylons. The bare flesh showed through, above her knee. Soft skin.

"If we'd planned on running out of gas, I guess we would've worn our walking shoes." Charlene, the one next to him, had a sharp tongue on her. Smart-aleck, she was. Ought to be more grateful for the ride.

She smiled as if to make up. "You think there's a payphone anywhere nearby?"

"Hard to say. Maybe at the gas station." They'd be wanting to call their husbands to the rescue. He nodded toward Evvie. "What about you, little missy? Cat got your tongue?"

"What's that thing hanging from the mirror?" She glanced at the rearview mirror where a small clay skull encircled by a miniature wreath of bright yellow flowers swung on a braided turquoise string.

"Kinda strange looking, isn't it?" Wilbur Sands smiled. His Dia de los Muertos memento. He didn't mind it, her nervousness. "What do you guess it is?"

Charlene spoke up. "It looks like Halloween, or something to scare little kids with." She said it like a taunt.

"I don't think it's scary," Evvie said. "Just weird."

"It's a remembrance," Wilbur said, a tiredness nudging at him. "An offering for the Day of the Dead. Those yellow flowers on the skull? They're marigolds to honor them that's passed. My nephew in Arizona sent it when my wife died." It made Wilbur feel better about things, the little skull, a reminder of Rosie. It merely observed—no judgments, no talking—that knowing stare on its face.

"I'm sorry," Evvie said. She sounded sweet, sympathetic.

"When I seen you girls, it made me think of how I'd feel about my Rosie out here all alone."

"You're a good man, Mr. Sands," Charlene assured him.

He wasn't so sure about that sometimes.

~ ~ ~

You'd have thought Abby would have been watching for him, but Wilbur was forced to climb out of the truck and go up to the door and knock. A chorus of deep-throated barks rounded the corner of the house as Wilbur mounted the front porch steps. Abby's curs must be tied up, else they'd be slavering all over him. The cool dusk ran up his exposed forearms. The cab of the truck had warmed up, the windows steamy from the two women inside. Even after he'd dropped them off at the filling station, he had to mess with the defroster to try to clear the windows. Now, the late afternoon was chilly, and the damp didn't help any. He'd warm up some when he unloaded the wood. Probably gin up a sweat again slaving on his own. Made him mad already, the thoughts of Abby in front of the TV while he worked his butt off.

Abby swung open the front door. "You finally made it." The warm light of the living room, the flicker of the TV spilled out onto the rough planks of the front porch. "Thought you weren't going to show." Abby was short and about ten years younger than Wilbur, despite his sparse hair and furrowed forehead.

"Told you I'd be here." What an asshole, Wilbur thought.

"Ask him in." Wilbur heard Dell's voice call out from inside.

"Aw, he probably wants to get unloaded and on his way." Abby stood squarely across the doorway. "Right, buddy?"

"You got my parts?"

"Need you ask?" Abby laughed at him. As though he knew that Wilbur knew the whole deal had a big chance of falling through. As though it was funny Wilbur had loaded up all that wood up and drove forty-five minutes in the rain not really sure if Abby would live up to his end of the bargain.

"Your phone's out." All Wilbur had to go on was Abby's assurance the previous week that he'd have the parts from his brother-in-law by this weekend. Wilbur had given him a specific list of the exact parts he needed, written down so there'd be no reason for Abby screw it up. When Wilbur tried to call and confirm yesterday, all he got was an out-of-service message. No surprise; it was out as much as it was on. Abby always had some sort of excuse: they lost his payment, Dell forgot to pay the bill, their mailman was a no-account who stashed the outgoing mail in the woods when he wasn't of a mind to make the trip back into town.

"Ha. What else is new? Those fools at the utility company." Only half an excuse this time. Abby stepped out onto the front porch. "Come on. You can unload at the back of the barn. I'll show you. I've got your stuff in the basement."

"I'm not unloading till I know you have my parts."

"Hey, you don't trust me?" Abby laughed again, slapping Wilbur on the shoulder. "Come on. I'll help you unload." He placed his palm on Wilbur's back trying to move them away from the door and off the porch.

Wilbur stood stock still, his boots solid against the porch's uneven planks. "Abby. I'm telling you." Wilbur's arm twitched. It was all he could do to not grab him by the neck.

Abby lowered his voice, confidential, man to man. "Look, I don't want Dell to find out. I promised her I wouldn't get her brother mixed up in any more of my deals."

But Wilbur didn't trust Dell any more than he trusted Abby. His jaw tightened. "Just get the parts for my truck." Like he expected. Weaseling out again. What ticked him off most was he could never prove Abby's deliberate intent to screw him over, his excuses always at least halfway plausible.

"Okay, okay. Hell, if you don't want me to help with the wood . . ."

That damn Abby. Wilbur was stuck with the loaded-up truck one way or another. If they were going to make the deal, Wilbur would get better than expected if Abby helped with the wood. Wilbur needed those parts so he could get his corn out. It would be April in a week. He'd lose precious time if he was left to hustle up another buyer.

"Forget it. I'm not fooling with you." Wilbur stepped out from under the porch eave into the rain. "I can get good money for this wood."

"Nobody needs firewood in the spring, old buddy." Abby grinned.

Wilbur stopped and thought, I could take him down.

Abby laughed. "Hey, I'm jerking your chain. I'll go get your stuff. Dell's watching TV, so I'll bring it up through the kitchen and out the back door. You can pull up to the barn." Abby turned to go inside then looked over his shoulder. "It's good to see you, buddy." And he disappeared into the house.

The time hadn't changed yet, and the weather brought on an early dusk. Wilbur parked the truck on the right side of the decrepit barn. Even his own barn looked to be in better shape. The closest place appeared to be under the overhang against the south-facing wall, not the back of the barn, like Abby said. Might as well get at it before dark took over. Considering he'd split the wood, loaded the truck, and driven near on an hour up to Hamilton, Wilbur was way more than halfway in at this point. He'd get his truck parts one way or another. And he'd stack the wood here, just to spite Abby.

Wilbur got into a rhythm and he'd emptied the truck about two-thirds of the way by the time Abby showed back up with a cardboard box.

"Hey, what are you doing? I said the back of the barn." Abby peered from under the hood of his rain jacket.

"Doing you a favor." Fool, Wilbur added to himself. "It's protected here; the wood's going to dry better." Wilbur motioned to the box. "Here, let me see that."

Abby set the box next to the back bumper and Wilbur peered in, moved aside the seals, counting. Two seals, three gears. Wilbur looked up. "There's two gears missing." Shoulders tensed, his blood rolled towards a slow boil.

"Who's counting? How many gears does it take?"

"I gave you the list." Wilbur saw things slipping away. Again. "I gave you a list, goddammit." He lunged at Abby, grabbed hold of his jacket.

"Aw, man. It's not my fault." Abby tried to move away, slipped in the mud, and started to fall backwards. He snatched at Wilbur's arms to catch himself, pulling Wilbur down with him.

"Let go of me, you queer." Wilbur fought to get away from Abby's awkward embrace and they both rolled into a muddy patch. Down there in the muck of dirt, rain, and moldering leaves, it flitted through Wilbur's head that he could easily shove Abby's face into the slime. Hold it there till he sucked the mud into his mouth, into his nose. Till he smothered.

They both struggled to stand and Abby slipped again. Wilbur heard a thud. He stared down at Abby lying there still as an old rag doll. Wilbur leaned in to take a closer look. Not a twitch and then a low moan. Abby slowly made it to his knees and then holding the back of his head, he stood, groaning still.

Abby jerked his hand away from his head with surprise on his face and peered down at his hand. "I'm bleeding. I told you it wasn't my fault, and you assaulted me."

"It's never your fault, butthole." Wilbur took a step toward Abby. "I warned you the last time."

"Stay away." Abby raised his hands and edged backward towards the house. "You'd better get out of here. I'm calling the sheriff." A braver tone, once he'd sidled out of Wilbur's reach.

Wilbur turned and stalked around to the driver's side of his truck. "Your phone's not working, asshole."

As he pulled the truck door to, he heard Abby yell, "It was off the hook!"

~ ~ ~

The rain petered out to a drizzle, and by the time Wilbur reached the turn off from the state highway headed towards home, every bit of wet had been wrung from the sky. The clay skull grimaced at him, lit by the dashboard light. Not as friendly-faced as usual. Wilbur hadn't expected much from the day, and he hadn't been disappointed.

A third of the firewood was still piled in the back of the truck. Maybe he could persuade Charlie Proctor to buy it off him and the day wouldn't be a complete loss. And he'd taken off without his truck parts. He'd have to wait and see if the sheriff showed up. Probably an empty threat, except you never knew about Abby. It wouldn't go any better than the last time, if the sheriff did come round.

He crushed the butt of his cigarette against the metal tab of the truck's ashtray. The pain had crept back into his knuckles. I helped those women, though, he thought. They were city girls, but the rain had evened things up. He probably could have made some kind of impression on that dark-headed girl if there hadn't been the two of them. Two changed things.

He pictured crunching over the gravel driveway and Rosie waving at him from the front porch, the windows a warm glow behind her. That, instead of a cold, dark house. He'd tell her about Abby—what a snake. Tell her how he almost punched him out but kept his head. How he stacked the wood on the side of the barn, not where Abby said.

Jamie Elliott Keith lives in Knoxville, Tennessee, where she writes and volunteers in the community. Her poetry has been published in a number of journals, and her first chapbook, "Past the Edge of Blue," was released in October 2017, by *Iris Press*. She is working on a series of short stories set in Tupelo, Mississippi, in the late 1960s to early 1970s.

Amanda Barusch

Once

I was a girl not a nymph just a girl; a chapped-hands-pinning-sheets-in-the-breeze kind of girl with a secret love of soaring. Some girls (beloved of painters) glide and gaze coy to the right; blue vein pulse at the temple and a single pearl centered at the base of the neck. No, I was of the bouncing ones, cracked at the heel, pulling fish bones from my teeth, guzzling wine in the afternoon—intact, but not untouched. I soared, but I did not glide, and

I never should have soared within sight of that bow-legged demigod with his bulging groin, and bulbous nose. He was not as artists draw him—smooth, clean, and symmetrical. No, he was randy as a porcupine with lead chains and that sibilant claim of affection. He found me *charming in disorder*, said he could see through my dress.

Of course, I ran. Anyone would have, but no one was fast as I. I am a god! He screamed in my wake. He moaned, pled, and finally gave chase. My hair tangled and streaming, and no one fast as I, but he drew close and his fingers grazed my scattering hem. I called out to mother for rescue and my rescue began in the loamy space beneath my fingernails. Insidious tendrils lodged there, plunged into my skin, and sent fresh leaves out to reach for the glimmering sun. I sense their fanning still, in the ghosts of my fingertips. Rough tubers burst from my heels. Like bloodhounds, they sought the most fragrant earth. Dragging my splintered body (twigs in my hair), they dove down to anchor my bleeding soles to the ground. My blood dried. Bark encased my breasts. The chords in my neck swelled and stiffened 'til my head bent back, eyes wide to sun and rain. My teeth clattered while the blood cooled in my veins. He stood clinging to my trunk.

No one else noticed. It was so quick, or it was so slow. No one human could see.

He's gone long ago. The spring sap flows and my leaves tremble. Tiny feet stream down the path below. My roots throb to their beat. The wind carries hints of skin and scented hair, as their warm sighs drift to the canopy.

One comes close to pluck at an arrow someone whittled in my winter bark. Small, sturdy, with an essence of rosemary, she leans on my trunk and kicks the ground. Echoes wave through the field. Then she pushes off and slips down the path, leaving a warm patch on my trunk.

I groan, sway, and toss a leaf to light her way.

Amanda completed her MFA at the University of Utah and has published fiction and poetry here and there. She is working on a novella called Being Impossible that seeks to reclaim the ancient myth of Fenrir.

Moss Ingram

Losing Sides

On the outside

the young man is rigid, sitting in a pew inside the small church

his friend lies in the casket at the foot of the small stage

he pretends to listen, their sentiments spray his ears like BBs misting a
   tungsten drum

he is well-trained, having also quit the wrestling team for all their talk
   and torment

On the inside

the young man has had enough of all the talk and crying

he stands and maneuvers his way to the foot of the stage

the preacher pauses and stares, the murmuring congregation
   crescendos to a communal gasp

nothing can stop him from lifting the lid

On the outside

he endures all the sideways glances, stoic and calm, having seen and
   heard it all

he kneels and lowers his head, closing his eyes when he is supposed to
   pray

On the inside

the young man is certain that if he cradles the back of Michael's head

Michael will blink himself awake and they will laugh together as they

    flee the church

On the outside

the young man has retraced where Michael walked barefoot, deep into

    the woods

he has seen where his friend wore his blue pajamas late one night and

    waited

listening for a reason to return to bed, to wake up in the morning like

    any other

instead of cradling his father's favored waterfowl shotgun

On the inside

the young man pretends to pray, squeezing his clammy intertwined

    fingers together

he hears the cacophony of winter tearing away the last remnants of fall

    from the trees

he sees Michael kneeling in the icy wet muck of leaves

he feels himself grasping at the clumps of soil underneath

Moss Ingram earned his MFA from Queens University of Charlotte and his Certificate in Advanced Studies in Design and Innovation Management from Kendall College of Art and Design of Ferris State University. He is the recipient of an honorable mention from *Glimmer Train*, co-recipient of an Edison Award for Innovation, and he has workshopped under such luminary writers as Margaret Atwood and Chuck Wendig at the Pelee Island Bookhouse in Ontario. Over the past 30 years, he has worked as a freelance writer, reporter, columnist, cartoonist, and writing consultant. He is the author of several books on technology, primarily used by Fortune 500 companies, and he has held a variety of editorial roles. Throughout his career, he has completed innovation projects for organizations as wide-ranging as the United Nations and the Internal Revenue Service and is regularly invited to consult on the development of new products and services, provide design critiques, assess and judge new business ideas for innovation competitions, as well as to serve as a guest speaker and panelist to share his thoughts on innovation and design thinking methods, sustainability, and writing. He lives in Grand Rapids, Michigan with his wife and two children, where he is an associate professor at Grand Rapids Community College.

Alle C. Hall

Dressed Left

The bird said, What color are my eyes. The cock scratched his balls—he dressed right—and he said, Doesn't matter. The bird said, Fooey, tied on an attractive bonnet, and flew in search of a cage.

The next cage was lined with heretical thoughts. She could spend years here, but her parents were pulling the worms. They agreed to pull for four years. And, they insisted, their birdy would live in a big, safe, cage with lots of tweety birds. The bird said, Fooey, bought a Jackie O. hat, and flew to The Sorbonne, where she met a French fox who dressed left. He shat prose poems. He introduced her to rooms full of radiant parrots and glamorous flamingos. How wren-like she felt, amidst their artistic intellectualism, their sexual politicization.

Mais non, cherie, they cooed. It was polymorphous non-perversity. It was the end of rectilinear thought.

I prefer merely to fuck, said her French fox. Defying stereotype, he stayed faithful—aside from that one time at Burning Man that he begged her to help him win the Beaver Eating Contest.

The bird thought, "We need a little more *normal* around here." As you see, she re-instated the use of quotation marks and flew to South Korea, where she quickly found a cage in which to teach English. It was boring but well-paid—and teaching English in Japan was soooo 1980s.

Alle C. Hall is the Senior Nonfiction Editor at JMWW Journal. Her work appears in *Tupelo Quarterly, Creative Nonfiction Magazine, Brevity (blog), Treehouse, The Citron Review, Bust, Literary Mama,* and *The Stranger* (Contributing Writer), among others. She won first place in The Richard Hugo House New Works Competition and was a semi-finalist for both *Hippocampus'* "Remember in November" Memoir Contest, and *Screencraft's* Cinematic Short Story Contest. She received a Best of the Net nomination from *Word Riot,* and two "Notable Essay" designations from *Memoir Magazine's* #MeToo Essay Contest. Alle blogs at About Childhood: Answers for Writers, Parents, and Former Children.

Christina Dalcher

Weeknights at Café Suicide

It was lovely watching them die.

Mostly, I thought as I set the tables—Spode Stafford Flowers for Mrs. Stansbury's hen party, ultra-modern Mikasa geometrical for Mr. Ashton (a walking dictionary entry for 'spoiled frat boy'), crazy Sally Carmichael's own handmade pottery for her group of six—it was lovely getting paid for it. Without Tuesday nights, the bistro I'd been running for nearly a decade on my own would have bled itself out of business.

Euthanasia cafés had been popping up around the city selling everything from fifteen-dollar design-your-own ramen bowls, to fusing Korean with Tex-Mex with Nova Scotian, but I'd always been—in Mark's words—a stubborn old bitch. So fuck the trends, I would stick with the classics.

I laughed as I laid out plates and arranged silverware, remembering how squeamish I'd once been.

~~~

"I couldn't," I'd said ten years ago over a batch of Hollandaise. I'd managed to avoid boiling it into a mess of yellow curd—barely.

Mark dipped in a pinky, tasted the sauce, and nodded his approval. "You're one hell of fast learner, Janie."

I had no choice but to cram four years of culinary school into the four months Mark had left to live.

"Let's work on the consommés and estouffades now," he said, decanting my Hollandaise into a storage container. His hands shook as

24

he sealed it closed. "Nail them, and you're golden. And, by the way, yes you can."

What Mark thought I could do wasn't listed in the index of his soup-stained and spine-cracked Guide to Modern Cookery. Escoffier had a recipe for everything—except murder. I told him again I wouldn't do it.

"Euthanasia," Mark said. "It isn't murder if the victim wants to die." Then, pointing to one of the bubbling All-Clad saucepans on the six-burner stove, he added, "You need to stir this. Until your arm falls off."

I looked at Mark's arms, the ones that held me tight on the Ferris wheel that night he proposed, the ones I sank into when he returned from a year-long stint in Paris brushing up on his continental butchery skills. Most of the muscle had softened from lack of use, and Mark's culinary adventures consisted of rolling himself from stove to fridge to pantry, supervising me while he still could.

The hallucinations were the worst. And they always came at night.

"Did you take your meds?" I said, glancing at one of the three kitchen clocks.

"Of course."

Mark now consumed a daily cocktail of antipsychotics, but those first nights, when he woke up in a sheet-tangled sweat, were unforgettable. Lying beside me, he screamed of the bisque tasting of gasoline, or the crème brûlée smelling of the burnt flesh of infants. Each evening invited a new chapter in the nightmare edition of Larousse Gastronomique.

And there was the time I woke to him standing over me with a knife. Some nights, it would be the cleaver from his sacred bag of cutlery; others, it might be a paring knife. The one that frightened me most, though, was the fine blade of the filet knife. I'd seen him use it on countless trout and salmon, prying away skin from meat and bone with the skill of a surgeon.

Maybe that was the first time I thought of it, staring up at Mark's shadow-darkened face, moonlight glinting off the steel. "It's me, honey. It's Janie." I said my name until the sounds ran together, Janiejaniejaniejaniejanie, until, finally, he put the knife down and sank onto the bed, sweat sticking to his body in a thin, sticky film.

He'd only gotten sick after what should have been a simple operation.

~~~

Tuesdays were my busiest times; only two of my staff had the nerve to work the private parties. Kate, a young blonde with more curves than Monroe, served; Emma, small and dark and more of a perfectionist than I, assisted in the kitchen. Neither of them had any hang-ups where death was concerned, although a faint shadow of something I couldn't quite place darkened both of them, a shadow I thought out of place on such young girls. I never asked questions, and they never volunteered answers.

Kate also doubled as my sommelier, curating the carte du vin and guiding the guests in their selections, some of which would be the last wine they ever tasted; Emma wrote out the menus in fine calligraphy. Tonight, while Mr. Ashton and Sally Carmichael would be content with pinot noir and a modest sauvignon blanc (Sally was so goddamned cheap), Mrs. Stansbury's request had Kate hopping. The old bat wanted elderberry wine; said it reminded her of 'those bygone days.' Whatever. They were paying me oodles. If they wanted fried sheep's balls and Schlitz on the rocks, I'd give it to them.

So far, all of my Tuesday guests happily chose from the menu. A tomato aspic would start Mrs. Stansbury's party, followed by a consommé Florentine (I had steered her toward this soup, thinking the chicken and spinach might serve as a pleasant foil to the tartness of the aspic). For the entrée, Kate would serve poached trout on a bed of parsleyed white potatoes. It was a plain dish, but who would want to give Mrs. Stansbury heartburn at her last supper? I was an opportunist, but no one could call me unkind.

"How are the crêpes coming along, Emma?" I said, checking over my sous chef's shoulder as she shook and swirled a shallow pan of batter.

Emma flipped the pancake, thin as gossamer, with the same flick of her wrist Mark had made me practice a thousand times. "Last one, chef. They're gonna love these."

They'd fucking better, I thought. Two bites of Emma's crêpes Suzette would be the last thing Mrs. Stansbury ever tasted. Her guests would finish their plates, assuming they still had an appetite.

Death has been known to put a damper on such things.

"And the sauce?" I said.

"All finished." Emma chuckled. "Well, mostly. Kate will straighten it out at table after she does her fire thing."

"Flambèing," I corrected, and checked the clock near the stove where Emma worked. Quarter to six, it said—only thirty minutes until the Stansbury party arrived. "Where's Kate?"

Emma tilted her toque-covered curls toward the dining room. "Setting up out there."

I called Kate in and reviewed the plan for this evening. Make sure she's comfortable. Keep the water and wine flowing. Offer to take a photo if they want. "And remember, flambè first, serve the others, and then tip the bottle over the chafing dish." I demonstrated, palming an empty glass vial in one hand while making stirring motions with an invisible spoon in the other. "Don't let them see you."

Kate nodded. "Got it, Janie."

Mrs. Stansbury would be easy. The Ashton party, on the other hand, had demanded plated desserts, which meant getting the order sorted out in the kitchen. It also meant drumming the system into Kate's pretty little head. No one wanted a repeat performance of last year's screw-up—it almost drove us out of business. Worse, Kate's mistake with the Boudreaux family might have sent me to prison, if Alain Boudreaux hadn't been so understanding when we accidentally killed his wife instead of him. Legal or not, there were still regulations, rule number one being Don't Kill the Other Guests.

"She didn't have much time, anyway," Alain had said, holding his lifeless bride of fifty years. "Francoise knew it, but she couldn't bring herself to see things my way." There, amid their children and grandchildren, he had asked me to prepare a second plate of fraises Chantilly, with an extra helping of cream. Fifteen minutes later, Alain Boudreaux had been as dead as his wife.

I remembered him smiling as he had spooned up the laced strawberries, holding Francoise's ringed hand for as long as he had the strength to do so. The children wept as Kate and I cleared nine dessert plates, and Kate herself wept when, back in the kitchen, I laid into her next to a pair of stainless bowls smeared with remnants of whipped cream.

"How could you screw this up?" I'd screamed.

Kate had blubbed something about the china all looking the same. "Mrs. Boudreaux was supposed to get the rosa and salvia plate, but I gave her the one with rhododendron and prinsepia. I'm so sorry."

I wiped the two switched plates clean. Kate was right—they did all look the same. Fucking Spode.

After the Boudreaux incident, we started marking all the special servingware with an unmistakable cross of blue masking tape on the bottom of each plate. Emma had suggested a black X on the rim, but I killed that idea. My guests didn't need a reminder that their savarins and soufflés were laced with a lethal dose of sodium pentobarbital.

"Well," I said as the girls unmolded shimmering aspic onto a silver platter, "at least the Ashton party will be too drunk to notice. Put an X on Mr. Ashton's plate." With that, I set about touring the three private dining rooms that would host our Tuesday evening parties.

~~~

Mark's last supper hadn't been at the bistro, but at home in our own dining room. He'd insisted—when he could still insist—on an exact replication of the 1903 menu served to President Loubet, a post-opera party that, in Mark's words, would prove me a master of all things Escoffier.

"Turn this one out, Janie, and I'll die a proud man," he'd said, stroking my hair with a trembling hand as I pored over the ingredients list. My husband was dying, and all he was interested in were glazed quails and crayfish mousse with a side of petits pois.

"Stop talking about death," I'd said.

But we both knew it would happen. Mark had three good months, on the outside. After that, the degeneration would have been too far along.

Spongiform, the surgeon had told us. Form of a sponge. I hated those words almost as much as the man who spoke them.

Mark's brain, Dr. Fletcher had explained, was in the process of turning into a mass of hole-ridden tissue as defective proteins ate their way through his cells. Five other patients had been infected; all were dead by the time of our meeting.

"How did that happen?" I asked.

Fletcher shifted a little in his leather chair. He was a stocky man with iron hair and a fat face that wore a permanent flush. His next lines sounded like a well-rehearsed monologue. "There were complications with your husband's tonsillectomy." He checked his notes. "This past March. The risks were all enumerated in the waivers he signed prior to admission. And, of course, the Board has reviewed the case, as well as the standard procedures for sterilizing surgical equipment. I'm so sorry."

That was it. That was what passed for an explanation and an apology. He might as well have told us what a pity it was a few loose prions on a pair of forceps transmitted spongiform encephalopathy among the six patients he'd operated on that spring morning. So sorry your husband has Mad Cow Disease, ma'am.

Sonofabitch.

We left Fletcher's office without shaking his hand, and I never saw him again.

Until a week ago.

~~~

I walked slowly through the main dining room, which would remain empty this evening as my Tuesday guests always dined in private nooks. That benefit was included in the price. Still, Kate had taken pains to set the tables, turning them out with fresh linens and flowers, straightening any wayward chairs, and filling salt cellars with pink and gray crystals we imported from Normandy. Salt from France, pentobarbital from the pharmacy, I thought.

I supposed we could have accommodated the few regulars who might drop in, but the survivors often used this main room to congregate after the business was done. At a cover of a thousand dollars per diner, I was happy to give them their privacy.

On the way past table nine, I noticed an ugly crimson stain on the silk wallpaper, just to the left of the four-top.

Kate shook her head. "Nasty bunch of assholes, those guys. If they show up again, can you serve them? One of them actually asked me to sit on his lap. 'How about a ride on the pleasure train?' he said. As if anyone could find his thing in all that fat."

I remembered the party, mostly because I remembered Fletcher's face. He'd grown a pair of jowls since that day in his office, but he was still as florid as he was ten years ago. If I hadn't been struggling to pay the girls, I'd never have served Fletcher. Or I'd have dished him up a purée of Alpo and called it mouse au chien.

"That bad?" I said to Kate.

"Awful." She pointed to the chair nearest the stained wallpaper. "Drunk as a fucking skunk. That's where the wine stain came from."

"If they come back, let me handle it."

Kate began sorting the menus for tonight's parties. "And another thing. They all had beepers. The fat guy's kept going off. Beep. Beep.

30

Beep. I mean, like constantly. I told him no cells were allowed in the restaurant, and you know what he said?"

I shook my head.

"He said 'I'm a doctor, sugar-britches, and this isn't a cell phone, it's a beeper. It's called being on call, so why don't you move that perky little ass of yours and get my guests another bottle of wine.' Swear to god, that's what he said. Word for word." Kate wiggled her ass. "You think it's perky? Anyway, the bottle of wine—it was their fourth—wasn't for his guests. The fat guy drank it all."

"As perky as a ninth-grade cheerleader," I said absently. What I was thinking was that I would definitely not be serving Dr. Fleltcher again, budget be damned.

By Friday night, I'd be eating those very words.

~~~

Mark had finished every bite of his last meal, save the dessert, a dish that was supposed to be Pêches et Fraises Sainte-Alliance. The peaches and strawberries weren't a problem in the late summer, but neither one of us had any idea what an alliance sauce was, saintly or not. I made two bowls of peach Melba as a substitute, lacing half of the raspberry purée with ten grams of pentobarbital after dissolving it in a sugar solution.

"Stay here with me?" he said.

"Of course." All it had taken was a half-hour with Google to convince me Mark's way was the right way. You eat, you sleep, you die. Better that than spending your last month as a blind vegetable with the jitters. And I'd had four months to get used to his plan. I didn't like it, but the alternative was unthinkable. No one survives what Mark had. No one.

Mark picked up his spoon with a trembling hand, then set it down again. "I need to know you'll be okay," he said. "You and the bistro."

"You want to talk about business? Now?" The raspberries topping my dessert had all the appeal of clotted blood, and my own hands

31

shook more than Mark's. "Screw the bistro. I'll let two of the girls go and run it myself. We'll manage."

He took up the spoon again and started eating around the edges, avoiding the sauce. If he didn't do it now—right now—I'd take the plates up and throw the whole mess down the sink disposal. "Janie, I think you should apply for a euthanasia license."

I listened, first in horror, then in absolute disbelief.

"So," he said. The vanilla sauce and peaches were now stained a deep scarlet, and he paused. "Think of it. Cancer, HIV, Lou Gehrig's disease, multiple sclerosis—who wants to live with that shit? All you'd be doing is giving them one hell of a sendoff. And they'd pay, Janie. They'd pay."

"How much?"

Mark looked up at the ceiling as if it had turned into a giant chalkboard, and I watched him work through the numbers. "The noodle guy on Main Street charges two hundred fifty a head. "

"You're kidding. For noodles?" We'd eaten there once, when we couldn't stomach another bite of unsold goose liver pâté. I remember seeing the empty ramen packages in the dumpsters out back.

"For the drugs, Janie. For the drugs."

Mark poked his spoon at me. "You could charge them a thousand a head. Party of eight means you net—I don't know—seven thousand. And they get a bargain. You could do a few groups a week. Say on Tuesdays. Tuesdays are shit in the restaurant business."

They were. Everyone knew that.

He took my hand and leant over the table. "Promise you'll think about it?"

"I'll think about it. I love you, Mark."

"Love you more," he said, scooping up a heaping spoonful of peach and vanilla and raspberry. "Remember what we talked about."

I hated watching him eat, but I'd promised. And I knew the story I'd tell when the time came to make the call. It would be the same story family members of my guests would relate years after—the Boudreaux kids, Mr. Stansbury, Ashton's handsome young friends, Sally Carmichael's pottery group. All of them. With every relation singing the same song, self-euthanasia was a matter of some medical examiner signing on the dotted line.

On his third bite, Mark's speech began to slur. His grip on my hand slackened and I had to feed him the rest of the peach Melba, one poisonous mouthful at a time.

It was done. Mark slept, I grieved, and the coroner signed off on suicide.

~~~

Mrs. Stansbury was the first to die tonight.

She went peacefully, a dribble of orange butter from her last bite on her lips as six blue-rinsed bridge players dabbed at their eyes and mopped up their plates with Emma's perfect crêpes. Sally Carmichael went next, at exactly eight-twenty-three, a number she deemed auspicious because the digits added up to thirty-one.

"Why thirty-one?" Kate asked as we cleared the ceramic goblets of mousse au chocolat from the Carmichael party's table.

"That's how many years she's been turning out pottery," I said.

Kate picked up another misshapen plate, all angles and scallops. "We did the art world a service, Janie. She needed about thirty-one more."

"Don't speak ill of the dead, Kate," I said at the time. Later, in the kitchen, I thought about Kate's words. It would be a service, and one the right kind of people might be willing to pay for.

Like Dr. Fletcher's dead patients.

Kate came storming in. "They're still not done upstairs. It's eleven o'clock and they want a round of brandy before dessert. Christ." She began filling a tray with snifters.

"What?" I said.

"It's worse than that. I don't think Mr. Ashton's ready to go." Kate popped off a shoe and began working the muscles in her right foot. "I mean, they only have the room for four hours, right? I need to go home and let the babysitter off."

The plates in the sink could wait. "I'll talk to him," I said, and headed upstairs.

Mr. Leonard Ashton—Lenny to his friends—glowed with a light I hadn't yet seen in the terminally ill. Five individual plates of the Charlotte Russe à l'orange I'd slaved over all afternoon sat untouched in front of each guest, the dessert's once sturdy lady fingers growing limp before my eyes. Lenny's pentobarbital-laced serving had been pushed toward the center of the table. He held court with the same fussy pedantry he'd used on me when reviewing tonight's menu, apparently not having registered my presence at the door.

"And I told her," he said, "I wanted the salmon poached until it was just flaking. Just flaking. Stupid bitch. No wonder this place is empty most nights."

Kate arrived with the tray of snifters and a decanter of Armagnac.

"Is that XO?" Lenny said.

"VSOP, sir. I'm sorry, but this is the only Armagnac we've got. It's very good."

He waved it away. "I only drink XO." Then, to the four men at the table, "See what I mean?"

Kate turned to leave.

"And take this mess back to the kitchen," Lenny said, pointing to the Charlotte Russes.

"But sir—"

"Are you deaf?"

I stepped into the room. "Is there a problem?"

Lenny enumerated seven of them, one for each of the courses he'd been served. "I'm not paying a cent for this shit," he said. "It's dog food at best. We got better food from the fat cook at our fraternity house."

My blood started to boil. I wasn't Mark, but I was still the best chef in town. I'd put the noodle guy out of business in my first month, the Tex-Mex place in my second. It took every ounce of self-control I had in me not to fling the uneaten charlotte in Lenny's face. "Payment has already been charged to your card, Mr. Ashton. As your contract stipulates."

"Fuck my contract. I'll take it up with American Express."

Five thousand dollars down the drain, I thought. Most of the money had already been spent restocking my supplies of barbiturates.

Before I could open my mouth, Lenny hit me with his version of how the game would play out: Either I would find him a bottle of Armagnac XO in the next fifteen minutes, cancel his card payment, and get the hell out of his room, or I'd be spending the rest of my days in a brick hotel cooking institutional quantities of shit on a shingle. He pushed his dessert in front of the smirking frat boy on his right.

"I'll say you screwed up the order. That clear?" he said. "Meantime bring us another two of these." He shook a nearly empty bottle of wine. "It tastes like piss, but it's got alcohol at least."

"As crystal." I nodded to Kate and we left the room, Lenny and his guests laughing behind us.

"That one's an asshole, isn't he?" she said on the way downstairs. "All of them."

It took me ten seconds to make up my mind. I gave my car keys to Kate. "Go to my house. Call your sitter on the way and tell her she's staying the night."

Kate started to protest.

"Tell her you'll pay her five hundred. That should shut her up." I gave her instructions on where to find the booze in my house. "Make sure it's an unopened bottle," I said. When Kate was out the door, Emma and I went to work with a pastry brush on the brandy snifters, painting them thickly with a clear coat of death.

Lenny's party had turned into a drunken brawl by the time Kate reappeared with the Armagnac.

"How about a little lap dance, baby?" Lenny said, his voice thick with the last of my pinot noir stock. He picked up his phone and held it out. "Or I make a call and you can help your boss dish out prison food for the next fifty years. Unless you get the chair, of course." Another roar of laughter filled the room as Lenny circled Kate's waist with one arm and grasped the back of her head with his free hand. "Dance for me, honey. Now."

The men began thumping the table with their fists. "Dance, dance, dance," they chanted. One of them raised a glass and drained it dry. "My turn next!" he said and flung the empty crystal at a wall.

Kate's eyes widened with fear.

"At least let her pour the Armagnac," I said. "Then you can do whatever you want with her."

Lenny grabbed the bottle from the tray, considered it, and pushed Kate off of him. "Fill 'em up, girl, and then come back here. I'm not done with you." He looked at me. "Leave. We'll take the room for the rest of the night."

"Of course," I said, and left them, standing outside the closed door until I heard five solid thunks.

~~~

Kate, Emma, and I buried them in my backyard.

"Two of them are still breathing," Kate said.

I checked five pulses before rolling Leonard Ashton's party into the trench we'd been digging all night. "Five, actually. Do you care?"

"Nah," Kate said. "They were jerks. Same as that doctor the other night." She paused as if remembering something unpleasant. "And my ex-husband. Sonofabitch sent me to the hospital once because we'd run out of beer."

Emma stiffened. "I'm never getting married. Not to a man, anyway."

A low moan came from the pile of bodies. It was Lenny.

"Asshole," Emma said, and kicked him once, twice, three times. Then she rolled him into the mass grave and dusted off her hands. "He looks like a guy I knew once."

We backfilled the gaping hole with dirt and rocks until our backs were sore. In my kitchen, over tea and shortbread, Emma spilled everything.

"He lives here now," she said. "Two streets away from me. One day—that time we ran out of cream and I had to go to the Giant, I ran into him. He asked me out. Like he didn't even know who I was. Like he didn't remember getting me drunk and fucking me in his dorm room. Can we kill him, too?"

I poured another round of tea and smiled.

~~~

It had been Mark's idea and was now my business. Tuesdays for the self-euthanasia crowd, Wednesdays for the vengeance jobs, and Thursdays for the frat boy rapists and wife-beaters Kate lured in with promises of a good time for all. We had a few regulars in over the weekend, mostly older couples who talked about how Julia Child changed their lives and how they'd rather hear her say "Just give it a good whack!" than watch that foul-mouthed British guy or the one who says "Bam!" every ten seconds. I charged them almost nothing for a nine-course tasting meal that rivaled anything they could get in Paris.

We started with Dr. Fletcher, Kate's ex-husband, Emma's date rapist, and a five-pound box of Gopher Go. Pentobarbital was too kind; strychnine, on the other hand, had a nasty bite—two to three hours of painful, backbreaking convulsions and muscle spasms.

Emma did a hell of a job forging the contracts while Kate set up the private rooms and served bowls of rich boeuf bourguignon, coq au vin, bouillabaisse to our guests. We'd spent a fair amount of the earnings from our partnership soundproofing the private dining areas, but the money hadn't gone to waste, not when Dr. Fletcher and his party of three began to dig into their meals, when the drunk surgeon who had killed Mark started to twitch and jerk and gasp. I put my arms around the girls after we served the next two rooms.

It was lovely watching them die. Slowly.

Christina Dalcher is a linguist, novelist, and flash fiction addict from Somewhere in the American South. Find her sometimes prize-winning work in *The Molotov Cocktail, Whiskey Paper*, and *New South Journal*, among others. Her debut novel, "VOX," will be published by *Berkley/Penguin Random House* in August 2018. She is an active member of International Thriller Writers.

Karen Zey

Lesson in Hugs

Parasympathetic Balance

The physiology of hugging works like this: hugs lasting 20 seconds or longer release oxytocin into the bloodstream, helping to regulate the nervous system. Hugs induce feelings of comfort and personal security, resulting in lower blood pressure and improved cardiovascular health. Hugs are good for you.

Innocence

When I was a little girl, my father scooped me up in his arms in the front hall as soon he came home from work. He held me against his chest, right next to his beating heart, and asked me what I had done that day at school. I rubbed my palm against the scratchy bristles on his cheek and whispered my tiny triumphs in his ear. Inside my father's hug, feet dangling midair, I imagined all kinds of futures.

Loneliness

A Montreal man offered free hugs to strangers in a subway station. Was he tired of sitting alone in his room listening to *Eleanor Rigby*? On the evening news, I saw his shabby cords, his bushy beard, his bilingual green T-shirt with chunky white letters: Câlin Gratuit/Free Hugs. He spread his arms to passersby, inviting them to enjoy a fleeting moment of human connection. Transport authorities did not agree that indiscriminate hugs, even if asexual in nature, were better than none. They fined him for giving away comfort in a public place.

Language of Lovers

In the early stages of romance, hugs pulse with desire. I remember my lover's arms entwining my body with heat just before his mouth found mine. I remember our late morning after-hugs in twisted sheets. After years of marriage, my lover-now-husband enfolds me in the warmth of longstanding love. A walk-by squeeze in the kitchen, a quick hug before leaving for work. When I toss and turn beside him in bed, his arms reach for me in a half-asleep hug, that moment of nighttime intimacy still so sweet.

Exceptions

Not everyone likes being hugged. Dr. Temple Grandin, a woman with autism and a PhD in Animal Science, invented a squeeze machine for herself. The deep pressure of her hugging machine calmed her atypical nervous system and reduced her anxiety. I heard her speak once at an autism conference. Temple Grandin's words shone with humanity. Sadly, the woman thanking Dr. Grandin put her arm around Grandin's shoulder in a casual half-hug, making her flinch in front of all those people. Recoiling from hugs is not always a sign of a miserable childhood.

Natural Order

My son loved to cuddle as a toddler but shrugged off my hugs as he grew into teenaged life. I clung to his childhood as he got ready to launch into his own space. The day he moved to his first apartment, he gave me a bear hug in front of all of his buddies. He headed off with them to figure out Ikea instructions and feast on pizza and beer. He comes home for dinner most weekends, and even when I don't offer left-over pot roast in Tupperware, he hugs me goodbye every time. Precious au revoir hugs in my empty nest.

Heartbreak

I hugged my friend when she walked away from a bad relationship. She packed up her belongings, snuck away when the SOB wasn't home, took her red eyes and wet cheeks across town to a new house. At the end of my one-week visit, we stood at my departure gate in the airport, and I wrapped my arms around her in sisterly support. Her body trembled against mine as I tried to squeeze away her self-doubts, her second thoughts, her fears. I gave her one final hug, tight enough and long enough to last, because you can't hug over the phone.

Solace

After her stroke, my 92-year-old mother languished in a nursing home bed, silent except for her wheezy breaths. Day after day, as the hours ticked away, caregivers moved their hands over her withered body, turning her, washing her, feeding her. When I visited, I leaned down toward her pillow and draped my arms around her shoulders. Her gaze fluttered towards my face. Vague recognition? A weak spasm of memory? Even though she couldn't hug back, even though she was dying, I believe my mother knew I was there.

What to Remember

Science explains the workings of the limbic brain. Human touch, like a poet's words, reveals the fullness of life.

Karen Zey is a Canadian writer from Pointe-Claire, Quebec. Her work has appeared in the *Brevity Blog, Cleaver, Cold Creek Review, Hippocampus, Memoir Magazine, Prick of the Spindle, Proximity's "True"* and other places. She received her first Pushcart nomination in 2015. Karen is currently working on a memoir about her many years teaching and consulting in special education.

Eli T. Mond

The Death of a Dancer

Narrated by The Desert in Which She Passed

In these formations, I lied, an ocean;

My only companions, you and the belly

Of the serpent that struck your thigh

—there was a keen dissonance in its rattling.

If only you could've heard its warning,

If only your grace had followed you here.

You used to be a dancer—a songstress of the body—

With feet like fluttering flutes

And arms reaching for a purpose beyond

That of those carnal hymns

You'd grown so used to singing.

You'd fallen into the swelling shade of a dune,

Drifting off into a dreaded slumber

Induced by the venom that danced to the rhythm

By which you'd lived your younger days.

In my arms, you dreamed your final dream;

And from your lips, a wistful song was whispered:

"Is death a lonely thing like me?

A sole vibration of ivory and string?"

Eli T. Mond is the pen name of David Davis, a writer, artist, and mystic from Detroit, MI. He is the Founding Editor of *Hyperlimenous* (f.k.a. *The Ibis Head Review*), a contemporary art and culture webzine, and has had work published in various journals, including *OTHER.*, *Lyceum*, *Occulum*, *Crack the Spine*, and *Young Ravens Literary Review*.

Jim Breslin

In Lieu of Flowers

In lieu of flowers, please wear a Hawaiian shirt to the memorial service. Or a funny t-shirt. Wear sandals with your cargo shorts. Slip into torn jeans and well-worn Converse sneakers. Keep it casual. While in line, tell a joke to the stranger in line behind you. Laugh.

In lieu of a charitable donation, treat yourself to a piece of art. Visit a gallery and purchase one drawing, painting, or a photograph that stops you in your tracks. Browse through a craft fair and pick up a multi-colored knitted wool cap, a beaded bracelet, or a piece of stained glass. Rummage through yard sales until you find a kitschy ceramic sculpture that makes you smile. Put the art on your walls, the sculptures on your shelves, the hats on your head. Hang the stained glass in the window that gets the morning sun. Enjoy.

Remembrances may be made by taking a mental health day and sleeping in. Read a poem before rolling out of bed. Make yourself a greasy cheese omelet and home fries while your favorite rock 'n roll music blasts through the kitchen. Dance in your pajamas with a mimosa in your hand. Take a vow to use all your vacation time. Later in the morning, stop in at your local used book store. Rummage through the shelves slowly, noting the titles and authors. Smell the worn pages and tattered covers. Choose a torn paperback you wouldn't normally read, preferably one with a tawdry cover and a subversive plot. Conspicuously read your book at the local coffee shop. When finished, scribble a personal message inside and drop the book into your local little free library box.

In lieu of lighting a candle, stop into an indy record shop and ask the tattooed woman behind the counter, the one with the nose ring, what pop-punk vinyl she has on her turntable. Look through the bins and buy an album from an obscure young band with a funny name. Listen on repeat. Find the rhythm. Memorize the lyrics. When said band comes to the dank basement venue in the city, buy a ticket. Study the band photo so you can say hi when the drummer walks by. At the show, bang your graying head in unison to the hipsters. They won't mind. Breathe in the humid air, inhale the fragrant communal sweat. Stand at the edge of the mosh pit and watch the kids dance in rhythm to the music. When the scrawny kid stumbles, reach out. Lift him back to his feet and hand him his lost sneaker. He'll high five you with a smile. Drink in the frenetic energy. As the purple haired girl in a flannel shirt dives off the stage, hold up your hands and catch her. She trusts you. Observe the unabashed joy on their youthful faces. In this moment, they are alive. You can be too.

Jim Breslin's writing has appeared in *Hippocampus, Schuylkill Valley Journal, Turk's Head Review,* and other journals. He is the author of "Shoplandia," a humorous novel about the working lives of show hosts, producers and crew at a home shopping channel. Jim is the founder of West Chester Story Slam, and the co-founder of *Lancaster Story Slam.* He lives in West Chester, PA.

Linda Boroff

Angie Gets a Job

Angie was not qualifying; she was crying. With one hand across her eyes, she groped for the tissue box that her interviewer extended without looking up as he checked her typing test. From between her fingers, Angie watched him circle errors; the sharp red pencil reminded her of a bird's beak: peck, stab, scratch. It left bloody little wounds all over her page. This abysmal performance confirmed every pessimistic prediction of her destiny that Angie had ever heard in her seventeen years.

"Miss uh, Morris." The man, gray-haired, with swinging wattles and rheumy brown eyes, held the flimsy page at a slight distance, like a soiled diaper. "You type thirteen words per minute, once the errors are subtracted." Angie ducked behind her tissue. "We cannot very well hire you as a typist, now can we?" He arched his brows, as if seeking agreement.

"But I must have a job!" Angie wailed. A child still, she believed in the magical power of her own needs to drive the decisions of others. "Or... or else I have to move home." This was a lie. In fact, Angie needed a job precisely because she was not permitted to move home. But she didn't dare confide in this grandfatherly personnel director. That would open a window on her past even more prejudicial than her terrible typing.

To Angie's surprise, her inquisitor hesitated at her mention of moving home, and she, with the canny intuition of the delinquent, sensed a weak spot in his perimeter and pushed on through.

"I'd be so ashamed in front of my parents. I moved out to live on my own and now I'm failing." Her head drooped, and her long, curling black hair swept forward to obscure her face, which rather disappointed her interviewer. He liked gazing at the pretty thing in her cheap gray cotton skirt — two runs in her hose — and worn red sweater. Charming. But hopelessly unqualified. She huddled penitently before him, peeking out from her tissue with reddened blue eyes. Angie's distress seemed sincere enough. And anybody who needed work as badly as she did would surely strive to improve her typing skills.

"Well," he said with mock reluctance. "I'm going to go out on a limb." Angie's heart gave an extra, tripping little beat. "I'll hire you conditionally. But..." he frowned, stern as Jove, and Angie's eyes widened in flattering response, "you must raise your typing speed to forty words per minute" (the eyes grew huge) "within three months. If you can do that, you'll go on permanent status." Caught in mid-sniff, Angie searched his face. Her grin blazed out like the sun from a ragged rain cloud.

"Oh, Mr...." she glanced at the black and gold nameplate, "Mr. Trueblood! I don't know how to thank you. Oh, I'll work so hard."

"I'm sure you will, Angie." For a moment they beamed almost conspiratorially at one another, and into Mr. Trueblood's mind suddenly flashed the word "snookered," although that did not diminish the width of his smile.

Angie danced out of the office past the scowling old receptionist, who handed her a packet of employment forms with the trepidation of a cold war operative passing classified information to a suspected mole.

Since this was Friday afternoon, Angie now had a whole weekend to luxuriate in idleness and dissipation. She knew of a party Saturday night. And she had a date on Sunday with a man she met at Larry Blake's Rathskeller on Telegraph Avenue, where she and her roommate Kati were drinking on fake IDs. The man, who confessed to being forty-two, claimed to own a gull-wing Mercedes and a luxurious home in the Oakland Hills from which his wife had recently exited. The anticipation of a restaurant meal and all the liquor she could hold made Angie euphoric as she jolted along on the bus back to Berkeley.

For weeks, fear and uncertainty had kept Angie awake at night. While her roommates slept, she would sneak into the bathroom and weep, rocking back and forth on the seat, wiping her eyes with toilet paper. Only yesterday, Angie had dialed her mother collect from a pay phone and received a histrionic response. Mrs. Morris, an inventory clerk in a Los Angeles department store, had her hands full just supporting Angie's younger sister, Frances. Even now, Mr. Morris was refusing to pay child support for Francie, in defiance of a court order. The woman he lived with hung up on Mrs. Morris when she called. You have to get a job like everybody else, her mother shouted.

And now, when all hope had fled, Angie was saved. Her roommates, Kati and Maryellen, could reinstate the phone, cut off due to Angie's arrearage. And they could finally give the air to Butch, their pesky landlord.

For the last two months Butch had accepted two-thirds of the rent, on the assurance that Angie was seeking work with the determination of an Everest summiteer. But since the girls owed him money, he had taken to dropping by and hanging around, asking suggestive questions and snooping through the rooms, "inspecting" for bogus leaks or electrical shorts. He complained that he was in trouble with his wife over their rent. Butch had a crush on Kati, who was Hungarian and beautiful. If Kati was home when he came by, she had to pretend to leave in order to get rid of him.

Maryellen had curly, platinum blonde hair, a deep dimple in her chin, and heavy thighs. She wore no makeup, which made her look washed out and churchy. But when Kati had suggested a little mascara, Maryellen just snorted.

Maryellen's brother Kyle, who studied psychology at the university, had taken Angie on a movie date the week before. When she got into his car, Kyle had pulled his penis out of his pants and driven like that through the city streets all the way to the theater. Angie, uncertain what to do, had chatted away nervously about Berkeley, politics and such. All the while, out of the corner of her eye she could see Kyle's penis bumping along like a third, silent passenger. When they reached the theater, Kyle had zipped himself back up and the evening had proceeded quite normally.

In the car on the way home, Kyle took himself out again, which Angie had kind of expected. Upon arriving, she had leaped from the car and thanked Kyle for the movie. He bid her good night amiably from behind the steering wheel, still exposed.

When Angie told Kati about the date, they agreed that Kyle seemed weird, but neither could say for certain what was truly aberrant among college men.

"I think Kyle is a pervert in the making," said Angie. And Kati must have reported that to Maryellen, because Maryellen shortly thereafter quit speaking to Angie at all. Nights, she would sit knitting on the couch, addressing her comments to Kati as though Angie did not exist. The bitch, thought Angie. She reminds me of Madame de Farge in *A Tale of Two Cities,* counting her stitches. "A Tale of Three Girls," Angie thought, composing a story in her mind. Secretly, she yearned to be a writer. But Angie's new job only carried her farther away from her dream, and nobody seemed to care.

Angie needn't have worried about raising her typing speed. She was in demand at Croft & Comstock the way fresh recruits had been in the trenches of World War I. The company's East Bay headquarters was located off Webster Street in downtown Oakland, in a five-story building as grim and practical as a penitentiary. A gray-walled reception area held only a green metal desk; the door behind it opened into a cavernous arena containing countless rows of desks eight abreast, with an IBM Selectric typewriter and a woman at each station. At opposite ends of the floor were the glassed-in cubicles of Mr. Kincaid, the manager, and Mr. Caverley, the East Bay Regional Director.

The typists ranged from teenagers to veterans whose backsides had broadened over the years to fit the office chairs, solid foundations for their atrophied upper bodies. Their arms served only to connect the torso to the gnarled and calloused hands, the fingers hammered spatulate on the QWERTY keyboard. The office was lit from above by fluorescent lights that cast a chill, greenish glare on every blemish, wrinkle, and scar.

Promptly at 8 a.m., the Selectrics hummed to life with a deafening clatter that lasted till five. And weren't they all lucky to have today's advanced technology? Not like in the old days, declared Marie, the pool's champion typist, when their fingers would crack and bleed after hours of pounding the manual keys.

Marie had been with the company for fifteen years. She had a way of sliding the keys together in a sort of arpeggio that generated line after smooth line of perfect type like black cuts across the paper. She was the Vladimir Horowitz of credit report typing.

Marie had an unhappy home life, as did most of the typists. Men tricked the women into bed, spent their puny wages, beat, cheated, and abandoned them. Merciless rigor kept the office superficially calm, but beneath was unstable magma. The younger girls had not yet learned the lessons of discretion; they trusted one another with their hearts' secrets and were regularly betrayed. Screaming battles and deep simmering feuds erupted.

Mr. Caverley, gray and flinty, took little notice of the typists, reserving his conversation for the younger manager, Rich Kincaid. He relished humiliating Mr. Kincaid, delivering ripostes from the side of his mouth in a jocular, hearty way, so that Mr. Kincaid had to laugh along, as if he too enjoyed the jibe.

"Hey Rich," Mr. Caverley shouted suddenly above the din. The typists instinctively slowed to listen. "You got the March receivables bassackwards again!"

"I don't think so, Mr. Caverly." Rich Kincaid rose and sidled hippily across the office, through the too-narrow aisles, knocking papers, staplers, and files from the typists' desks. "What the deuce, get this stuff off here." A ripple of suppressed laughter followed his progress like a grass fire. The consequences of an outburst were too terrible to imagine—and that was dry tinder to the urge.

Mr. Kincaid took out his own rage on the women beneath him. No petty infraction escaped his notice. And he went beyond that. "Don't get caught late here with him," Angie was warned. "He'll be all over you." As if there were a chance of that! On the stroke of five, Angie was out the door, bypassing the balky elevator to race down the stairs two and three at a time.

At home, she exchanged her shabby dresses for jeans and tie-dyed shirts, wishing she could disappear into their infinite fractals. Then she and Kati cruised Telegraph Avenue, "looking for trouble," as they called it. Late at night, Angie might have to find her way home alone, crossing the dark campus, dodging through clumps of trees, hugging the shadows of buildings. By 7:30 a.m., she was at the bus stop in the early drizzle, wobbling on her high heels, eyes half closed.

One morning Angie looked up, and there was Mr. Kincaid in his new Oldsmobile, right at the curb. He smiled and waved, beckoning her into the car.

"It's my boss," she blurted. The other bus riders looked at her enviously.

"You waitin' for an engraved invitation?" shouted a tubby woman. "Wish it was me he was askin'." I do too, thought Angie, but a cold, rainy wind was whipping her thin skirt around her legs. She got into the car beside Mr. Kincaid, squeezing herself against the door to stay as far away as possible. The car was warm and smelled of leather.

"I didn't know you lived in Berkeley," said Mr. Kincaid.

Angie smiled with the corners of her mouth. "Do you live here too?"

Mr. Kincaid mumbled "Livermore," which was nowhere near Berkeley. Angie wished the Oldsmobile really could gobble up the street the way it did in advertisements. Each stoplight lasted forever; traffic was snarled.

"And where do your parents live?" asked Mr. Kincaid.

"L.A."

"My my, far from home." Well, thought Angie, here comes his hand on my leg. But Rich Kincaid said, "My son is dying, you know."

Angie blinked. "What?"

"He has a rare genetic disorder. I can hardly pronounce the name, even though we've been living with it for five years."

"I'm sorry," Angie said.

"Would you like to have dinner some time?" said Mr. Kincaid. "It's just... my wife has to be with Todd all the time. If his head is not held up, he can choke to death."

Mr. Kincaid had dark, thin hair cut very short, and sad brown eyes. He looked like a person whose son might be dying.

"How come you yell at everybody all the time?" Angie said suddenly, dizzy at her own nerve.

"I have a temper," said Rich Kincaid. "I admit it."

"Well it's not their fault."

"No," he said, "it isn't."

When they got to the parking lot, Angie let Mr. Kincaid kiss her and feel her up. He was so grateful he almost cried. They agreed that he would pick her up at her apartment from now on, so she didn't have to walk to the bus stop.

So Rich Kincaid drove Angie to work, and after a while he brought her home as well, and it was just as easy to stop for a bite of dinner on the way. Afterwards, they sat in the garage at Angie's apartment building and necked like high school kids.

"We're Catholic," he said. "I don't break God's law, just bend it a little to keep my sanity."

"Me too," said Angie, a wave of euphoric relief washing over her.

Every morning now, Marie looked sharply at Angie, though she and Rich were careful to separate blocks from the building and enter several minutes apart. Sometimes the entire typing pool was looking at her. So they know, thought Angie. So what? Whenever Rich hollered at a girl, he looked quickly at Angie, who tried to keep her features neutral. After work, he apologized.

"Don't say it to me," Angie turned away, arms folded. "Say it to her." But Rich never did.

Marie had a black eye. She didn't even try to put makeup on it, and everyone elaborately avoided asking her how it happened. The eye seemed to hover over the entire office as a dark and silent reminder: no matter how perfectly you typed, how punctual you were, how many rules you followed, it did you no good. The fundamental cruelty and unfairness of life could not be buffered or deflected.

Butch had a black eye. Kati's brother, Miklos, a fiery, brilliant graduate student who could not decide whom he loathed more, communists or capitalists, had been visiting on a Saturday afternoon, when Butch walked right through the door without knocking. There had been a scuffle, and Kati had screamed. Now all three girls were being evicted.

"You're our hero," said Angie to Miklos, who wore a tattered, oatmeal-colored scarf around his neck and whose shock of brown hair fell across keen gray eyes.

"He's not MY hero," said Maryellen, who had been trying to call Kyle, but for some reason their telephone was again disconnected.

"Maybe because Miklos doesn't whip it out the minute he's alone with a girl," said Angie. Maryellen charged and would have given Angie a black eye too, but Angie raced out the door and down the street. Dusk was falling, and a faint aroma of patchouli incense on the mild air gave Angie a sudden aching sense of life's ineluctable passing, of dreams abandoned. The old Victorian homes converted into student apartments looked wise and decadent and seductively inviting.

Psychedelic curtains hung at the windows; Country Joe and the Fish reached her ears: "Well it's one two three, what are we fightin' for?"

"I'm in love with your brother," Angie told Kati. "Please tell him I'd like to go out with him."

"Miklos would never go out with a typist," Kati replied. "That sounds cruel, but it's really kind. He would only use and discard you. Sex alone is meaningless to him. He is seeking his spiritual and intellectual equal."

"I'll go to school then," said Angie.

"He would never love a girl who got an education merely to snare a man," said Kati. "So it's hopeless."

"Hopeless," said Marie the next morning when Angie told her of this, "is what you are right now. Believe it or not, I once did the same thing with Mr. Caverly."

"Yuck," said Angie.

"If you can find a way to get out of here, do it. Before it's too late." Marie turned her misshapen body back to her keyboard.

Someday, Angie had once believed, all would come right, even if only in the kingdom of heaven. The just God existed transparently, so much a part of the usualness of things that his workings went unnoticed. In the end, though, all the good and deserving, living and dead, must at last heave a mighty sigh of relief and be at peace. But the truth was, Rich's son would soon die. Angie's father would never return. The typists would labor away, and love and prosperity would always, always elude them.

Angie sent for her high school transcripts and made an appointment at the University with an admissions officer named Trevor Beardsley. He was a young man with a prominent Adam's apple, long thin blond hair and a faint mustache.

"How can we admit you to the University of California?" Trevor said, holding Angie's transcripts at a slight distance. "You meet almost none of our academic criteria, plus you accumulated more than one hundred hours of detention for truancy."

Angie began to cry. "But my parents were getting a divorce," she wailed. "I had nobody to talk to. I didn't care about anything." This was a lie. Angie had cared deeply about a number of things, none of them having to do with school.

Trevor Beardsley looked around frantically for a tissue, but all he found was a crumpled paper napkin left over from his lunch. He offered it anyway, and Angie groped for it, one hand across her eyes. It's really a shame, Trevor thought, that the older generation had to lay their sick trips on their kids like that. Angie seemed like a very bright young woman. And anyone escaping from a Croft & Comstock typing pool would certainly study hard to keep her grades up. Trevor hesitated...

Linda Boroff graduated from UC Berkeley with a degree in English. Her writing has appeared in *McSweeney's*, *The Guardian*, *Hollywood Dementia*, *Drunk Monkeys*, *Word Riot*, *Hobart*, *Ducts*, *Blunderbuss*, *Adelaide*, *Thoughtful Dog*, *Storyglossia*, *Able Muse*, *The Furious Gazelle*, *JONAH Magazine*, *The Boiler*, and others, including several anthologies. She was nominated for a 2016 Pushcart Prize for fiction and won first prize in The Writers Place short story competition. She has written one feature film which played in theaters and film festivals in 2010. Her short story published in *Epoch* is under option to Sony and director Brad Furman (The Lincoln Lawyer) for development as a TV series. She wrote the script for the upcoming biopic of film noir actress Barbara Payton, currently casting with producer Don Murphy (Transformers).

Blake Kilgore

Emptying Too Fast

Our jeopardy was palpable when I was behind the veil. I held a weapon, but my vigilance was drowned by my restraint. *I don't want to hurt her.* She stabbed me twice in the heart and fled. I slumped against the stone and moss pavement, crimson pooling and spreading over my skin and into the fabric of my shirt, my organ in spasm from emptying too fast. Its pounding desperation was so loud that I woke. There was tightness in my chest, real pain. I'd been crumpled in a knot around her pillow, until the ache finally tore the shroud.

Blake Kilgore lives in Burlington, New Jersey, with his wife and four sons. People there treat him with kindness, and he is at ease living among the old and tall forests of the Garden State. His lingering accent, however, verifies that his heart is still Texan and Okie. Blake's writing has appeared in *Forge, Lunch Ticket, Midway Journal, The Stonecoast Review, Thrice Fiction* and other fine journals.

Domenic Scopa

House of Light

Above all the houses,

if you look hard, sweetheart,

stars are bleeding through

the black mesh of the night-sky.

Like patient listeners they wait

because you have something to say,

although you may not know it, yet.

We've memorized the love notes

stuffed inside our pockets,

like memories of sunrise,

but there's nothing

like the strength of darkness,

that caretaker of mystery,

and the stars, like glitter

thrown around at birthday parties

Before the birthday girl

unwraps a present

her face is the canvas of fresh snowfall

awaiting footprints,

the canvas of a river's surface

reflecting nothing

but the clear, electric evening clouds,

or the canvas of a brand-new mirror

covered with a bed sheet,

never to be gazed at.

The sky must think of stars

as scars, reminders,

and it desires emptiness

filled only with the possibility of sleep

I am the ashes of stars.

I wait for a breeze…

It doesn't come,

or I can't feel it—

But I'll tuck my chin and hope,

like always,

as I toss sunflower seeds to pigeons

clustered near the park bench,

and, someday I'll drop dead,

without warning,

like mating birds that plummet

in their blissful union…

Nothing ever ends, though.

During nights of bitter cold,

the moonlight disappoints you,

and the terrifying lovers

you begin to recollect

become me

Like an absent father,

I can't console.

The porch light dies,

and you disappear.

Somewhere, some creature

tips a garbage barrel.

Do you remember that cat

struck by the pickup?

By now a swarm of flies surrounds her.

Her struggle's finished.

So think of her purr.

Think of the stinging sleet

you looked at once, as a child,

through a window,

and then turned back,

double-checking that your door was locked,

that place of smoldering trauma,

where you only asked for safety,

and where no one was ever home

Except now, imagine

that on every surface there are lit candles,

their flames like flickering apostrophes,

so that house is,

momentarily,

made of light.

Domenic Scopa is a three-time Pushcart Prize nominee and the 2014 recipient of the Robert K. Johnson Poetry Prize and Garvin Tate Merit Scholarship. He holds an MFA from Vermont College of Fine Arts. His poetry and translations have been featured in *The Adirondack Review, Reed Magazine, Borderlands: Texas Poetry Review, Reunion: The Dallas Review, Belleville Park Pages,* and many others. He is currently a Lecturer at Plymouth State University and an Adjunct Professor of Literature at New Hampshire Technical Institute. His first book, "Walk-in Closet" (*Yellow Chair Press*), is forthcoming in 2017. He currently reads manuscripts for *Hunger Mountain* and *Ink Brush Publications.*

Timothy Gager

What Kids Are Scared Of

The Elvis's wig itched and smelled moldy as Artie slapped glue on it and palmed it onto place atop his bald head. He swung open the dented door of his Dodge Caravan, slammed a few pills, slung a stringless guitar over his shoulder and tried to process the decibels from a party of six-year olds around the back of the white house. "God knows I need the money," he thought. "No need to mention a cash job to the ex."

"Thanks for coming," Mr. Gladsphere said, pumping Artie's hand, placing three fifty-dollar bills in them. "Glad you work on short notice."

"Better that the clown wasn't available," Artie said. "A lot of kids are scared of them."

"Let's go," Gladsphere urged as Artie tried to walk faster, his white leather pants croaking against his large thighs. Did his wife leave him because of his large thighs? Did he lose his job because of them?

"Where's the clown?" Gladsphere's son Jimmy cried, when they arrived out back.

"Oh, it's the fat Elvis," great aunt Ginny said, adding one more to Jimmy's complaint while staring at Artie; close enough for him to notice the booze on her breath; her the booze on his. "I'm still a fan," she laughed at her own come on.

At Showtime, Jimmy's mother gave him the less than Vegas introduction but presented him as a special guest. The kids were silent, checking him out head to toe as if he were an alien, his large pant bells stiff as a board, and rhinestones twinkling like miniature burning bright headlights but certainly not like stars—never like stars. Artie was now *The King*.

Sweat rolled down Artie's chest like streams of rain against a window and then he jerked to life as the music began, "WELL, IT'S ONE FOR THE MONEY…TWO FOR THE SHOW…," he sang, and gyrated.

When "Blue Suede Shoes" ended, the Gladsphere's looked at each other, and Ginny's enraptured squeal was all the praise that rained. The children asked what Artie's name was.

"I am The King," he said. "You wanted The Clown but I am a king!" he said.

"I want a balloon elephant," Jimmy said.

"How about another song instead?" Artie asked in a southern accent; a Southern Jersey accent.

"I want an Indian headdress," some kid said. "A balloon one."

"Devil in Disguise?"

"A dog, a swan, a sword!" They all yelled at once.

Sprouting from the sleeve of Arties's white leather jacket, crinkly strands of the worn fringe limply dangled. They connected to the oversized cuff and the "hold that thought" finger he held up as he left the stage.

"Where do you think you're going? Is it too hot for you?" Ginny said in a sultry way, but Elvis ducked her, cutting around the corner of the white house and back toward the Caravan. "You'll never make it back," he thought, taking seven tiny white pills from his jacket and gulping them down.

Inside the van he looked for a bag of balloons, an air compressor and his white rubber clown face with orange hair, which flared upward on the side. He moved to his knees sifting through belongings in the cargo area. He started to throw them around; looking for all the things he had lost.

Timothy Gager is the author of fourteen books of short fiction and poetry. *Every Day There Is Something About Elephants*, a book of 108 flash fictions, selected by over fifty-five editors, was released by *Big Table Publishing* in 2018. He's hosted the successful Dire Literary Series in Cambridge, Massachusetts since 2001 and was the co-founder of The Somerville News Writers Festival. He has had over 500 works of fiction and poetry published and of which thirteen have been nominated for the Pushcart Prize. His work has been read on National Public Radio.

Perle Besserman

A Story in Stories

Chickens

I'm phobic about three things: confined spaces, dirt, and live chickens. Imagine, then, the shock of coming face to face with a slick, brown-feathered, mean-eyed rooster poised in attack mode in the corner of a dirt-encrusted Porto-Potty. Which is exactly what happened when, on a picnic with my soon-to-be ex-husband Erwin, I had gone off to pee in order to defuse an argument only to be confronted by my phobic trifecta.

I froze.

So, too, did the rooster.

We stood and stared at each other for what felt like a lifetime as images of my most terrifying childhood chicken encounter unspooled in the meager space between us.

It was summer, and I'd just turned ten and my sister twelve. (We were exactly two years and two months apart—my birthday was in July and Denise's in September.) Since there wasn't enough money for both of us to go to camp, it was decided that, being younger and easier to please, I would spend the summer at our grandparents' egg farm in upstate New York.

Those days nobody talked about "free range" versus "industrialized"; chickens simply milled around in the yard like Occupy anarchists in Zuccotti Park, pecking away at anything and everything in their paths: worms, seeds, bits of straw, an occasional corn kernel that had fallen from the feed pail Grandma Esty dumped into the trough in front of the chicken house where the hens laid their eggs. I avoided

64

chores involving the odiferous chickens and earned my keep by washing dishes and answering the phone if it happened to ring on a Sunday afternoon when my grandparents were napping. Grandma Esty, my father's mother, had never hidden the fact that she'd wanted grandsons and resented my mother for both "stealing" her son and producing only girl children, so I wisely stayed out of her way. A fanatic raw foods advocate, she fed me grapefruit with bran for breakfast and spinach salads for lunch. Suppers consisted of yogurt and an apple. Eggs were for selling, not for scrambling, frying, boiling, poaching, or eating. The only cooked food I tasted that summer were the Corn Dogs on a stick Grandpa Ian and I surreptitiously shared at a roadside stand when we went berry picking. My happiest days at the farm were those spent away from it on berry picking expeditions. Tutored in all things "outdoors" by my adored Grandpa Ian, I meandered through the woods alongside him distinguishing edibles from in-edibles and identifying trees and wildflowers.

But it was Grandma Esty who ruled the roost, in every sense of the word. She was tiny, stick-thin, and always angry, and I could never understand how it was that my tall and handsome, gentle grandfather could love her so tenderly. Then again, I was only a child and not yet wise in the crooked, uneven ways of love.

At first, I harbored neither fear nor interest in the chickens. The one exception was Bindy, a furious purple-combed "cock of the walk," a prolific stud of a rooster who, literally, had free range of the farm, strutting anywhere he pleased, at any time, and giving way to no one, human or animal. Like my grandmother, Bindy remained indifferent toward me as long as I kept my distance. That is, until the day the ball I was playing with rolled into the henhouse and I unthinkingly crawled in to retrieve it. Getting down on all fours at the entrance and holding my breath against the putrid poultry smell, I peered into the darkness. It was quiet, and there was no movement, so, feeling for the ball with my hands, I carefully inched my way inside—and was instantly confronted by Bindy's beady-eyed stare. Startled, I let out a hefty screech. Which was the worst thing I could possibly have done, for it set the rooster into immediate action. Defending his territory against what he must have taken for a competitor, or even worse, preparing to mount a potential mate, Bindy leapt toward my face, beak held high and aimed directly at my eyes.

Luckily at that moment I felt a strong, determined tugging at my ankles as my grandfather pulled me out of the henhouse feet first. Five seconds longer, and Bindy would have made short work of me, as my grandmother would later say when told of my misadventure—before adding that I had the makings of a "troublemaker" and no doubt took after my mother's side of the family.

Five and a half years of psychotherapy have helped me pinpoint the source of my sexually charged, highly contentious relationship with men to that summer day in the henhouse with Bindy, the raging rooster. As for the genetic component: I suspect my grandmother might have been at least partially right, for the one family member I came to resemble most, both in looks and behavior, was my mother's wayward brother Harry. Same thick, dark unruly hair, olive skin, black eyes, and bow-legged stride. The laws of genetics are Erwin's bailiwick, not mine. So, if you're looking for a hard and fast, deterministic reason for my becoming a phobic, troublemaking person forever unable to turn down a dare or stir up a fight, check with my geneticist ex-husband. Oh, and, in case you're wondering what happened next in my encounter with the rooster in the Porto-Potty that summer afternoon. I backed out the door and peed in the bushes before returning to find Erwin simultaneously packing up our picnic hamper and our marriage.

~~~

Uncle Harry

My grandmother wasn't entirely wrong about my genetic inheritance, just a bit off in her emphasis. For I can now say with some certainty that what she saw as "troublemaking" could more aptly be described as a shared spiritual restlessness with my uncle Harry.

The only boy in a family of four girls, born last to a mother in her forties, Harry was destined to be coddled by his sisters. His father Carlo, a Sicilian immigrant, had settled the family in Philadelphia and worked his way up from junk dealer to pizzeria owner. Harry's sisters had all been born back in Messina, making him not only special because he was male, but because he was the first child in the Stabile clan to have been born on American soil. The family pride and joy, his maleness so celebrated that at his christening party, guests showered the baby with gold coins specially provided for the occasion.

No surprise, then, that Harry became, as my mother put it, a "ladies' man." Adored, fussed and fought over, and fiercely protected by his sisters from early on, he fell quite effortlessly into that role. It was almost as if there was never a question that Harry could be anything but the focus of female attention wherever he found himself. Not that he was effeminate; his swarthy Italian looks mitigated against it. And the fact that he was a rugged, athletic boy known for telling smutty jokes and generously sharing the cigarettes he'd been smoking since he was twelve.

Never one for studying, Harry barely edged out of high school with a passing grade before signing up as a merchant seaman—which was how he made his way around the world and fell in love with a Chinese woman and her city, Shanghai. Mei Ling worked as a receptionist in the office of the shipping company that owned Harry's freighter, so she was the first person to welcome him on arrival and the last to see him off on departure. This coming and going went on for two years before Harry and Mei Ling were married by the freighter's captain, celebrating afterward with four of his mates and her widowed mother in attendance at a reception in the diplomat's room of a fancy hotel on the Bund. Harry continued sailing; Mei Ling remained at her job in Shanghai, their romantic once-a-year meetings eventually taking its toll on the marriage until one day Harry arrived to find Mei Ling no longer awaiting him on the dock with her customary covered dish of steamed sesame buns. When, after a month of numerous official inquiries, neither his wife nor her widowed mother was to be found anywhere in or around Shanghai, Harry began to doubt that Mei Ling had ever existed at all, that, like a seaborne fantasy common to sailors on long uninterrupted voyages, he'd dreamed her into being. Harry's leave was up, so he reluctantly boarded his ship and sailed back to the States. Unforeseen events intervened preventing him from returning to China, the most important of which was that the shipping company owner of the freighter was found guilty of illegally dumping waste at sea and went into bankruptcy, ending Harry's career as a merchant seaman. Fortunately, my uncle had taken no part in the illegal dumping and, after being questioned by the authorities, was free to go without being charged. Jobless, he returned to Philadelphia and went to work in his father's pizzeria. But Harry could not stay put for long and was soon traveling again. This time around the United States, selling subscriptions to The Reader's Digest book club. This brief but influential period in Harry's life turned him from a marginal reader into a voracious one—an addiction he passed on to eight-year-old me, when, after quitting his traveling salesman's job, he arrived at our door with the entire Reader's Digest library of books in the trunk of his car and dropping them off before leaving without telling anyone where he was going. It was only after Harry had returned to Philly two years later from a self-reported successful gambling stint in Las Vegas, investing his winnings in a pair of Fairmount row houses and moving into one of them with his new wife, my Aunt Peg, that I really got to know him. Or at least I thought I did. The fact is, I never actually knew whether or not to believe what Harry told me—about Shanghai, his Chinese wife Mei Ling, his career as a merchant seaman, or any of the multiple adventures designed to prove his extraordinariness. Aunt Peg didn't help clear things up, either. A redheaded showgirl with perfect melon-shaped breasts and long shapely legs, Peg soon relapsed into sullen invalidism, supposedly brought about by the unchecked disapproval of her husband's sisters, and avoided all contact with the family. When Harry came to visit us, in the Italian Market neighborhood, with expensive toys for me and my sister and cousins and outrageously priced bottles of wine for our parents, he did so on his own.

Fueling my discontent with the drab bourgeois ordinariness of the life I'd been born into, Harry—exaggerations and/or outright lies notwithstanding—became the model for everything I would aspire to. Which did not sit well with my father, who on more than one occasion referred to my uncle as "a four flusher" despite my mother's protestations. *

*(According to the online Urban Dictionary, a four flusher is: "Somebody who is obviously lying, posturing, idly boasting, who does not have the goods . . . Originally from game of poker, c.1880, one who bluffs that they have five cards in a flush when they only hold four.")

As a kid I lived in constant anticipation of Harry's visits and the lavish gifts he never failed to bring with him, my favorite being a red fire engine with a bell I could ring while riding around the block impressing the boys I longed to be friends with and alienating the girls with my tomboyish preference for mechanical toys over dolls and tea sets. Even more important for my mother and her sisters was the sorely lacking aura of glamour Harry brought into their lives. Not only had he managed to escape the rental apartments above and adjacent to my grandfather's pizzeria, where the rest of us still lived, but he'd already claimed a stake in the upscale gentrification of a far nicer neighborhood than ours. I remember the time he came to visit offering my father a share in his latest real estate venture, laying out on our kitchen table the renovation plans for three new row houses he was planning to buy. My father, a once-promising lyric tenor with frustrated operatic aspirations, had only just returned from his job as a post office clerk, and was annoyed at having to delay dinner when Harry, unannounced, rang the downstairs bell. Never inconvenienced by her brother's impromptu visits, my mother immediately began preparing for Harry to join us.

"I made your favorite—spaghetti and meatballs."

"Sorry, Kitty, but I don't have time. I just wanted to give you and Mike first dibs on this deal before showing it to anyone else."

My mother sat down at the table and, without even a glance at the blueprints spread out in front of her, started prodding my father. "It's a great opportunity to get in on the ground floor, Mike. Don't do your usual thing . . ." she looked up arching her eyebrows at my uncle, "you know how conservative he is when it comes to money, always misses out on a good deal. Penny wise, pound foolish."

My father reached into his shirt pocket, took out his glasses and, slowly, deliberately, put them on. "No need to rush," he waved her off. Then addressing my uncle, "How much money are you asking me for this time? You still owe me three thousand dollars for the last loan, you're aware of that, right?"

My mother sprang up from her chair. "You never told me . . ."

"Take it easy," my father said quietly, peering down at the blueprints.

Fingering the gold chain around his neck, Harry gave my father a shit-eating grin. "Okay, Mike. If that's the way you want to play, I'll take my marbles and go home." He reached out and started folding up the blueprints. My father pushed back his chair, and said, "Do whatever you want. I don't have the time, or the money, for this deal of yours. Besides, I'm hungry, and you know I don't do business on an empty stomach."

Seeing they'd both reached the tension high point that would inevitably give way to a shouting match, and possibly even worse, my mother dared not step in. And that, for at least the next three years, was the end of any possible partnership between Harry and my father. I'd been sitting on the floor, ostensibly engaged in playing jacks while eavesdropping on their conversation, burning to find out about that three-thousand-dollar loan and wondering whether my uncle would ever pay it back. Even as I got older, I was still too intimidated by their on-again-off-again "business" disputes to ask and didn't gather the courage to bring it up until years later, when my charismatic Italian uncle was long dead, and my short-fused Irish father was too old and demented to remember.

~ ~ ~

Adultery

It was said that Cervantes wrote Don Quixote to illustrate that reading too many romances could lead to madness. In the sixteenth-century, these action adventure stories-with-a-moral were all the rage. Ironically, Cervantes' cautionary tale had the opposite effect of what he intended, and Don Quixote became a romantic icon for the ages. I grew up at a time when books were still the best escape from the drab world of everyday reality, living proof of Cervantes' assertion that too much reading can indeed make you crazy—or "eccentric" at the least. From the day my uncle appeared at our door with his treasure trove of books, I went at reading with a passion, which, despite its unhappy consequences, continues to grip me still. Unlike the chastened Don, I was never cured of my romantic obsession. Unable to distance myself from what I was reading, I'd assume the imagined voices, accents, and gestures of my favorite characters. Carrying my fictional identity with me everywhere, I became "a heroine in my own novel," as my father took to calling me. When I'd read all of Harry's stash twice, and some even three times, memorizing entire swaths of The Good Earth, The Razor's Edge, and Lost Horizons, I continued feeding my not-so-secret addiction at the local public library. My arms piled high with the seven-storied tower of borrowed books permitted to card holders, I'd ignore the jeers of my rope skipping and ball playing sometime friends as I made my way home. By the time I got my scholarship to Princeton, I had devoured every book on the shelves from A-C in the Novels and Poetry sections and was determined to become a writer or die young.

Away from home, living inside the world of books made me an easy mark for predators posing as knights, so it was probably a good thing that Erwin and I married while I was still in college. Despite my book-fabricated sexually experienced persona, he was the first man I went to bed with, and for a time—thanks to my ensuing pregnancy and delivery—the last; not counting a brief dally with George, an Australian street musician I befriended on my daily outing with baby Victor in his pram. It happened at a time when Erwin always seemed to be working, often not coming home until after midnight. I was probably right in interpreting my husband's behavior as a sign that he'd lost interest in me—not that he'd ever really shown much to begin with. Reflecting on our relationship later, I realized that he'd probably married me out of a sense of duty. Erwin might have been a man lacking in feeling, but he was ethical to the bone—incapable of casting so much as a word of blame when I announced I was pregnant, not even after I admitted that I'd lied about using a diaphragm and didn't even own one.

George, on the other hand, was full of feeling, the ideal remedy for the Flaubertian role of neglected wife I happened to be playing at the time. Brutish yet sweetly naïve, in the way of Australian men who swing from tender to tempestuous depending on how many pints of beer they've imbibed, he literally wooed me with song. The first time I noticed him, he was seated against a lamppost in front of the gelateria on Palmer Square, his guitar resting in his lap, the scant assortment of coins in its open case reflecting his meager takings that day. He looked up at me and smiled his subway tile white smile just as I was passing by with baby Victor asleep in his pram. Stopping, I smiled back. George picked up his guitar and spontaneously serenaded me with Michelle, Ma Belle, and that was it! That he wore Doc Martens, black tee shirts and jeans and had long blond hair and blue eyes and looked like a younger version of my Grandpa Ian only added fuel to the initial spark of my attraction. In short, George, the Australian anti-Erwin who precipitated my first infidelity, succeeded because he was footloose, musical, and drove a motorcycle. Admittedly, superficial reasons for embarking on a month-long affair that, pleasant enough while it lasted, fizzled out in unforeseeable recrimination.

We established a routine, trysting on Mondays, Wednesdays, and Fridays in George's tiny furnished sublet on Ewing Street during the hours coinciding with Victor's nap. I'd park the pram in front of his two-story apartment building and, after making sure nobody was out on the street or at the windows, I'd carry Victor in his portable bassinet up the short stoop leading directly to George's door. Though it smelled of marijuana, the flat was always neat and tidy, the bed sheets freshly laundered and the bathroom sparkling clean. Not what I'd expected of my peripatetic Australian street musician, which for that reason alone made him even more seductive during those frazzled, unkempt days when I'd abandoned my own home to a depravity of roaches as I juggled caring for Victor and lovemaking with George between futile attempts to create poetry out of the mess I'd made of my life. My quickly fraying dramatic persona of the moment must have gotten on George's nerves, for, three and a half weeks into our affair, instead of serenading me in bed after an hour of tender lovemaking, he took to baiting me with testy discussions pitting the "academic" poems I'd made the mistake of reading to him aloud against the "spontaneity" he strove for in his music. When I defended my writing, he accused me of being "glib and pedantic" and launched into a diatribe against the university as "a den of phonies."

"Why are you saying this, to hurt me?"

"It's just the opposite, baby... it's 'cause I don't want you to become mediocre, like them. I don't want you to lose your edge, your passion."

"Right now, I don't have any 'edges'; you've filed them all down." Moving closer, I ran my fingers through his hair, thinking it might calm him. But it had just the opposite effect.

Pulling away from me, George said, "I always wanted to be a musician, but my parents wanted me to study law. They kept nagging me about it, so I left Melbourne Uni and went up to Brisbane and joined a band. "Frowning, he propped himself up against the pillows, his head thrust back, a strand of hair falling dramatically over his forehead. He pushed it aside, looked thoughtful for a moment, and then burst out laughing.

Unnerved by his sudden change of mood, I asked him what was so funny.

"You are, baby; you're funny," he looked at me, his clear blue eyes glinting like marbles.

"You're confused, and you're confusing me. You know what I think?"

"What?"

"I think you're using me to rationalize your own guilt about defying your parents and leaving the university."

"Could be, dahlin, could be . . ." Swinging his legs over the side of the bed, he got up and walked over to the window. "Sun's going down, time for you and Victor to go home," he said, letting me know it would soon be over between us.

Unwilling to own my rejection, I wondered if George's sudden dismissal indicated he'd been smoking too much pot—although I'd never caught him at it, and he'd never offered me any. It was only after he'd disappeared that I learned he'd been running a lucrative business dealing marijuana. A fact that surprised nobody else in Princeton but me! Evidence of yet another quixotic fantasy on my part: except that, unlike the shrewish, foul-mouthed tavern maid Dulcinea, my beloved object had appeared in the guise of a soft-spoken, sweetly singing minstrel.

Coincidentally, it was at about this time that Uncle Harry cheated on Aunt Peg with his lawyer's receptionist, "a plump, unattractive married woman who can't hold a candle to his wife." My mother whispered this information into the phone so as not to be overheard by my father, who'd "disowned" me for marrying while pregnant. Thanks to Harry's intervention, my mother and I had been in secret telephone contact since he'd sent her a photograph of baby Victor at six months. Knowing my father so well, and wisely judging that it was still too soon to attempt to heal the breach between us, my mother concluded that only after seeing the baby in person, at Christmas, when he'd been sufficiently "softened up" by the peace and good will of the season—

not to speak of two weeks of vacation from his tedious job at the Post Office—would my father be won over. Which is exactly how it happened.

Only now that Peg was at the receiving end of Harry's mistreatment and no longer resented for being beautiful and therefore "snobbish," could my mother admit her guilt at letting so much time elapse before opening up to her sister-in-law. I might have judged my mother more harshly if I weren't feeling guilty myself, because, like her, and all the other women who'd fallen under his spell, I was equally in thrall to Harry. But my mother was far more strong-willed than the rest of us, and, once she decided to take charge of the situation, even Harry had to knuckle under. As the family "diplomat," known for her skillful handling of squabbling relatives and litigious neighbors, she managed this latest crisis without involving her sisters (never an easy task when it came to their precious baby brother) steering a reconciliatory course between repentant husband and aggrieved wife—until Peg got out of bed one midwinter day and ran down the block barefoot in her nightgown announcing Harry's betrayal to any of her alarmed neighbors who would listen. Hospitalized with what was then diagnosed as a "nervous breakdown," Peg spent the following year in luxurious incarceration undergoing electroshock treatments. The first thing Harry did on her release was, take her on a Mediterranean cruise. After her second and third breakdowns and hospitalizations, and a diagnosis of "severe bipolar disorder," he moved her into an exclusive private psychiatric facility in Bryn Mawr, visiting regularly even after their legal separation had been finalized.

I visited Peg in the hospital twice. Both times, she'd been too heavily sedated to talk, but sat in the visitor's room holding my hand, refusing to let go when visiting hours were over and I'd gotten up to leave. By then, our hands were so sweaty and stuck together that a nurse had to pry them apart. When my mother called to find out how the visit went, I was too shaken to tell her about it, but the image of Peg in her armchair, staring at me with vacant cat-green eyes, her once abundant red hair cropped to the scalp, kept occupying my dreams. I was too cowardly to visit her in the hospital again, but that didn't stop me from merging her real mental suffering with my own largely self-created drama, starring George in the role of "Byronic hero" and myself as his love-struck devotee.

Haunted by the grim reality of Peg's descent into madness, I sought my usual escape in books. It was midwinter, and the East Coast was buried in snow. With the heat turned on full blast, I sat in my little home office with Victor in his playpen alongside me, immersed in the tempestuous world of Byron, my favorite romantic poet. But George's rejection had thrown me into such a frenzy of self-doubt that no amount of literary posturing could bring me out of it. Erwin and I were sleeping in separate rooms, an arrangement Victor grew to accept as "normal" even as he got older and found this not to be the case with his friends' parents. If he did notice something different about us, he never asked about it. The uncanny double of his father—same massive forehead, hooded grey eyes, and hunched shoulders, his genius guarded by the same impenetrable shield of silent disapproval—Victor, too, went off to Harvard at sixteen, differing from Erwin only in his choice of astrophysics as a major and an as yet undisclosed predilection for binge drinking. Victor's departure hit me hard. I'd grown accustomed to having him there as a buffer from despair. When he was a baby, and then a toddler, the everyday chores of washing, feeding, clothing, and playing with him had kept me from going over the edge on more than one occasion. Once he'd gone, there seemed to be no reason not to. I'd received my MFA with honors that same year and found a part-time teaching stint in the coveted New Jersey "Poetry in the Schools" program, from which I now had to take a leave of absence. Alternately depressed and manic, I knew I was in trouble when, one freezing winter day, I found myself standing on the platform contemplating an Anna Karenina-like leap in front of the approaching Trenton-bound train. Here I was, having married when I was barely twenty, with a child, and still only a stone's throw from my family in Philly, who everyone mistakenly took as the "good daughter" for staying so close to home—while straying off into adultery and contemplating suicide.

I'll say this for him; Erwin did manage to show some concern, and even went so far as to call Victor back home. But not before making me promise to seek out professional help. Put on long waiting lists by Princeton's entire population of busy psychiatrists, I became a hermit, spending entire days in pajamas barricaded in my bedroom, searching for salvation in spiritual self-help books, drinking endless pots of herbal tea and pausing only for toilet breaks. During those hermetic four weeks, I lost fifteen pounds. When I emerged, neither Erwin nor Victor appeared to notice; I could just as well have died and been transformed into a ghost. Father and son had managed perfectly well without me, fixing and eating meals together, watching television, laughing at each other's insider jokes. They went right on living as before—as if I weren't there. Then Victor returned to Harvard, and Erwin to his lab, and I was left to ruminate on the failed relationships with the men in my life.

Recipient of the Theodore Hoepfner Fiction Award and past writer-in-residence at the Mishkenot Sha'ananim Artists' Colony in Jerusalem, Perle Besserman's work was praised by Anthony Burgess, Gabriel Garcia Marquez, and by Isaac Bashevis Singer, for its "clarity and feeling for mystic lore," and by *Publisher's Weekly* for its "wisdom [that] points to a universal practice of the heart." She has written three novels, *Pilgrimage, Kabuki Boy, Widow Zion*, and a linked story collection, *Yeshiva Girl*. Her latest novel is *The Kabbalah Master*. Her short fiction has appeared in *The Southern Humanities Review, Agni, Transatlantic Review, Nebraska Review, Southerly, North American Review*, and in many other publications, both online and in print. Besserman's most recent books of creative non-fiction are *A New Zen for Women*, and *Zen Radicals, Rebels, and Reformers*, and *Grassroots Zen: Community and Practice in the 21st Century*,coauthored with Manfred Steger. She has appeared on television, radio, and in two documentary films about her work, and her books have been recorded and translated into over ten languages.

Lynn Marie Houston

Who Can Say What War Has Done

I have come to believe that an as yet undiscovered human need and even a property of matter is a desire for revelation. The truth within us has a way of coming out despite all conscious efforts to conceal it. I have heard stories from those in the generation after the war, all speaking of the same struggle to ferret truth from the silence of their parents so that they themselves could begin to live.

—*Susan Griffin, "Our Secret" (410)*

My students, in their teens and twenties, bend their heads over words they don't understand. I'm struggling with the essay, too, but not its meaning. I'm struck by how the author braids an autobiographical narrative of her 1950s childhood in America with an exploration of the devastation of World War II. My students and I read the rationale Susan Griffin gives in "Our Secret" for combining these historically incongruent topics: "I sense now that my life is still bound up with the lives of those who lived and died in this time" (383). The web of life. But how far does that web extend? I had my own secret about the lives that had touched mine, a web of connections that I was just beginning to see and understand.

Although I was teaching Griffin's essay in a freshman composition course, I was thinking of my own writing which had often linked my autobiography to a war I'd never known except in its aftermath. A handful of years before we'd opened our books in that classroom, I published an essay about my father's service in the Vietnam War whose title, "My Father's Secret," was so similar to Griffin's title, and whose main idea was also similar to Griffin's. I asked my students whether they felt that Griffin was permitted to claim a personal connection to a war she had only researched, had never seen firsthand. I asked if it was "ethical" for Susan Griffin to write intimately about the horrors of war when she had never served in the military, when she had never been in a firefight. And by asking what they thought about Griffin, I was really asking what they might think about me.

Predictably, the students' answers were mixed, ranging from someone who felt she had to defend her friends who had served ("It's just not right to pretend like you've seen something you haven't"), to others who stood up for Griffin's right to bear witness, not necessarily to what happened in World War II, they argued, but to its aftermath, its consequences that live on in the world. "A war like that," one of them said, "is everyone's responsibility." I felt my muscles relax, not even aware that they had tensed up in anticipation of their answers.

Earlier that day, I'd read a Facebook post by Siobhan Fallon, an author who writes about war and military life, sharing her frustration over a reader's Amazon review of her book *You Know When the Men Are Gone*. The reader had claimed that Fallon was trying to "get rich" off the experiences of veterans and had suggested that, as a civilian writing about military matters, she was disrespecting the people who have served in the Armed Forces. Fallon lamented the reader's ignorance about the economic realities of the book trade (in the post-Amazon, post-Kindle publishing world, writers make no money and presses are barely scraping by), and she mentioned that her intent was the opposite of what the reader claimed, that in writing about war she was hoping to draw greater attention to the suffering of veterans, to honor them by describing the events they lived through, their hard work, and their sacrifices. After all, Fallon is married to an officer in the Army and has been with him through several deployments. Also, Fallon's father, like mine, is a Vietnam veteran.

I don't bring up this question about who has the right to write about war purely out of an objective curiosity. I have a book coming out shortly from the Heartland Review Press, a book called *Unguarded*, which is a collection of poems made from the letters I sent to my boyfriend during his deployment with the National Guard. I am already at work on two more books of poems about veterans. And although I write about veterans' wartime experiences, I have never served in the military. What's more, unlike Fallon, I have never even been married to someone who has served. How close does my connection have to be to a veteran before I can write about war? Do I have to be someone's wife or does being a girlfriend count? Do I have to be a battle buddy or does being the daughter of a veteran count? I'm struggling to understand what gives me the right to imagine the things that veterans have been through in combat.

~~~

I sit across a table from my father's older brother. Over lunch, we're talking about some of the political differences in our family. My uncle's eyes dampen with tears as he tells me about the distance he feels now from my father: "We were so close when we were kids," he says. "I don't know what happened. I don't understand your father's politics or his love of guns." For months, I'd been trying to think of an answer for my uncle. And then, just a few days ago, my father gave me a folder that contained all the letters he'd sent home to his parents while he was serving in Vietnam.

In early December 1970, my father sends a letter home: "I have accepted the fact that I am in Vietnam and I will do my best. Even though it still doesn't seem possible."

I'm reading the letters my father sent home from the jungles of Vietnam. He writes the first few in his tent, after pulling guard duty all night, before he attempts to sleep through the hot afternoon. My father is twenty-two years old when he begins writing these letters. He will celebrate his twenty-third birthday somewhere north of Cam Rahn Bay.

On December 25th, 1970, my father writes "For me, it doesn't seem like Christmas. I really feel sorry for these people. They have nothing, except flies and mosquitoes. I hope this war ends soon."

My father turned seventy this past May. The people he addressed these letters to, my grandparents, have been dead for over a decade now. My father will tell you that he is not good with words, and my mother cannot talk about his time in Vietnam—she becomes incoherent with tears. Susan Griffin believes that "[t]o a certain kind of mind, what is hidden away ceases to exist" (404).

In January of 1971, he writes: "I am fine and have started counting the days. This place is not the most luxurious I have ever been in."

In 2006, four men are traveling through a desert in a Humvee when the vehicle hits an explosive device buried in the road. One man wakes up in a ditch with a concussion. Another breaks his pelvis. The driver has both of his legs blown off. The man thrown from the vehicle will lose part of his hearing and sustain permanent damage to his knees. Almost ten years after the explosion, I meet him through mutual friends. We date for a few weeks before he deploys again. I wait for him to return—write letters, bake cookies, wake up in the middle of the night to log on to Messenger. I count down the days in blocks of hours that seem to pass as slow as the molasses I watch fall into another bowl of cookie batter. I can't be there to help him through the difficult and stressful things he has to do, and he can't tell me much of what's going on, so I only feel better when I think I am making his living conditions better. Meanwhile, my living conditions deteriorate—I worry about his safety constantly; I don't eat well or sleep enough; I wake up with panic attacks. I think of all the things that would be better, more fun, if he were there to do them with me. Then I feel guilty about being so selfish. I wonder if my mother felt all of this when my father was in Vietnam. It was probably even worse for her.

When my boyfriend finally comes home, he becomes increasingly stressed about returning to his civilian job. After a month during which he snaps at me and blames me for things that couldn't possibly be my fault—the weather, the fact that cigarette smoking causes cancer, when he finds out a brewery he likes is closed on Mondays—he admits to having anger issues that require a therapist. On the day he is supposed to board a plane to visit me, to meet my father as he had requested, he breaks up with me, saying that he just can't be in a relationship, even though (I find out later) he's already seeing someone else. He never speaks to me again. How much is my life now affected by the wartime events he survived? How much is his story now my story? After he breaks my heart, I have trouble believing anything guys tell me. It takes me over a year to date again. How much of my happiness fell away as the man I would know as my future ex-boyfriend kneeled alongside a desert road and tightened the tourniquets he applied to his friend's legs?

My father writes, "Please forgive the dirty stationary. There is red dirt all over this place. This firebase isn't much, but it will be my home for a while."

On October 3, 2009, U.S. soldiers at Command Outpost Keating are involved in a 16-hour firefight called the Battle of Kamdesh. They lose eight men. Twenty-four more are wounded. One of the team leaders takes off his Kevlar, strips down to shorts and a t-shirt, and sprints around the base to locate all of the bodies of their fallen. He has shrapnel in his arm and a bullet wound through his shoulder. Sniper bullets strike the dirt behind him as he sprints. If they do not recover the bodies, the Taliban is likely to desecrate them and broadcast it on YouTube. Eight years after this event, I meet him at a bar in Nebraska, where I'm visiting for the summer. We date for over a month—late night conversations, texting for hours, laughter, future plans. Then, a week before I have to return to the East Coast, he blocks my number. No conversation, no explanation. He ghosts, and I'm broken hearted again. All I have left are a few memories, and they're not even very good ones. I remember waking one night to the jerks and twitches he was making in his sleep, trigger finger firing on top of the sheets. I remember wrapping my arms around him in the dark, holding him until the nightmare passed. A firefight in Afghanistan, a country I've never been to, has now become a part of me. And yet there's no term to describe my relationship to war. I've been touched by it, and yet I've never served. I've dated veterans, but never married one. I'm just a bystander. And yet, I've been shaped by the combat experiences that broke these men, just as they broke the men of my father's generation who went to Vietnam.

On January 12, 1971, my father writes, "I have been in the jungle for two days now. I cannot believe how heavy my pack is and how rough the terrain we have to go over. We will not get out of the woods for at least another 20 days."

Griffin writes, "Often I have looked back into my past with a new insight only to find that some old, hardly recollected feeling fits into a larger pattern of meaning" (382).

I've started to wonder how my father's service in Vietnam formed me as a child. And writing about it has been the means I'm using to explore this self-discovery. I remember an anxious childhood. Not deprived in any material way, nor lacking love. But I remember feeling "on edge," unsure whether my father's time in Vietnam was something to fear or something to be proud of. I possessed an understanding at perhaps too early of an age that everything good in our lives could be taken away suddenly. This was certainly the truth my parents lived when my father was drafted one month after they graduated college and got married. What our parents believe greatly influences us. Some biologists say that the trauma suffered by previous generations is passed down to us in our genes. Is this how as a civilian I have come to write about war? My father's contribution to my genetic composition? I gravitate now toward other people whose lives have been shaped by the notion that everything—our lives themselves—could be taken away in an instant.

Susan Griffin's theory is that "every life bears in some way on every other" (402). She believes that "the self is part of a larger matrix of relationship and society. Had we been born to a different family, in a different time, to a different world, we would not be the same. All the lives that surround us are in us" (411). I am a composite of my father's service; my mother's tears; the grandparents I hardly knew before they were gone; and the wounded, broken men I have tried, and failed, to love. Griffin explains, "For there is a sense in which we are all witnesses. . . The way of life we live, a life we have never really chosen, forces us to walk past what we see. And out at the edge, beyond what we see or hear, we can feel a greater suffering" (409). Why does writing about this suffering make a claim to owning it in a way that makes some people uncomfortable? If every act of writing requires empathy and imagination, how is it any different for writing about war?

Writers whose lives have been touched by war may not only have the right to write about it; they may have a moral obligation to do so. Civilians writing about how war has affected them build bridges to the experiences and voices of veterans, who may not able to tell their own stories. I recently attended an off-Broadway production that explored the difficulties military personnel and their families face when the former come home from war. As part of a panel discussion after his performance of *Outside Paducah: The Wars at Home*, playwright and actor J.A. Moad offered an inclusive definition of a veteran as "anyone who has been touched by war." I think Susan Griffin would agree. Every one of us who has had an intimacy with veterans as friends, family, or lovers are permitted to write about their wartime experiences with compassion, to help tell their stories from our perspectives, so that no one forgets the work it has taken to preserve the freedoms we enjoy, or the mistakes that have been made in their pursuit that have cost the lives of the dead and also the lives of some still walking, breathing, dating.

Lynn Marie Houston holds a PhD from Arizona State University and an MFA from Southern Connecticut State University. Her writing has appeared in numerous journals, including *O-Dark-Thirty, The Wrath-Bearing Tree, Consequences Magazine, Painted Bride Quarterly, The Ocean State Review*, and in her four books of poetry. Her work has earned distinction in contests sponsored by *The Broad River Review, Cultural Weekly, The National Federation of Press Women, The National Federation of State Poetry Societies*, and more. She has held writing residencies at the Vermont Studio Center, the Sundress Academy of the Arts, and the Art Farm of Nebraska.

Jules Gates

Raw Flesh and Bare Bones

I miss the vein-bulging, teeth-gritting, red-faced look of you

like you're going to tear some small live animal like me limb from limb,

and the growling, breathy, hoarse, and high-pitched squealing

of your attack and conquer,

the stealth silence, in dead black air,

stormed by a crash that slams into me and flips me three times over,

and when I land with a thud, breath knocked clear out of me,

all feet solid down on ground, a wild cat fury-possessed, fangs bared,

poised,

for more—and soft foot by padded foot, I stalk,

gasping for air, bloodied, battled, oozing, still prowling,

because the smell of you is the earth's original patchouli intoxicant,

complete with green, slimy, serpent with fire eyes,

and I want to slice it up like an apple, eat every morsel in tiny nibbling

bites,

with the scent slithering off my fingers, lips, and mind,

because, while I feast on you, it slides lithely and smoothly

inside my body and blood for eternity,

damned or not—(what the hell do I care?)

and I make you grow,

like the tree,

with veins, reds, thickness, wildly gigantic,

hanging with ripe, engorged fruit.

So what if you're my soul mate and I love you madly as just that—

a creature who appeared one day out of God's great blue?

Maybe I stole more than your rib.

And am not of you.

If not, I could worship you from afar as an Adonis, David, or Atlas,

(bearing oh so nakedly the weight of the world)

and fired and cured by my mythological maelstrom,

thrust out my Aphrodite-Valkyrie-Medusa claw

and throatily rasping, whisper like a vaporous wind…

"talk to this and nothing more."

Jules Gates is an Associate Professor of English in the Department of English and Modern Languages at Angelo State University, where she has worked with colleagues since 2002 on the annual ASU Writers Conference in Honor of Elmer Kelton, conducting the conference interview with Terrance Hayes in 2009, and chairing the conference for 2 years when Mary Karr (2010) and Art Spiegelman (2011) were the featured writers. Dr. Gates has published poetry in *Amarillo Bay*, *Blue Bonnet Review*, *Carcinogenic Poetry*, *Concho River Review*, *Voices de la Luna*, *Visions with Voices*, *Red River Review*, and several other Texas and US journals. She has presented poetry and creative nonfiction at the South Central Modern Language Association Conference, the Texas Association of Creative Writing Teachers Conference, and the Langdon Review Weekend.

Michelle Dotter

The Garden of Adonis

Death came suddenly to the Garden of Adonis. His brother sleep had passed through the ivory gates not long before, and he had set Ares off his guard, obscuring his mind with thoughts as flighty and purposeless as the gossamer bed sheets in which he and Aphrodite lay tangled, at the very center of another man's garden, the pivot of passion around which the whole earth spun. Ares leaned up on one elbow, watching Aphrodite skin an apple with her teeth, admiring the way the little curls of crimson fell like rose petals across her stainless breast and thinking that one or two rough kisses to complete the mirage might not be out of place when Aphrodite's eyes rolled back in her head. She shook against him, a mockery of their usual rhythm, and then slipped from the bed to crumple against the marble dais of her unwalled bedroom, one leg trapped beneath Ares at the edge of the pallet.

Ares watched her without moving. He did not worry because there was nothing to worry about. The lifetimes of men fell away in that silence, and until the garden began to die around him Ares did not move, watching Aphrodite on her back and waiting for the goddess to wake, or to resume breathing. A goddess could hold her breath for a very long time.

When the tree whose branches had always sheltered their bed lost its leaves for the first time, its deep roots parched by the decay of Aphrodite's love in the soil, Ares eased himself to the edge of the bed and let Aphrodite's leg fall away from him. Though he was god of war and fire, his blood ran cold at the hollow shudder of her unblemished thigh sliding down to join the rest of her on the deep white floor. He called her name but could not wake her. He touched her, but her skin was cold—the only time Aphrodite's heart had not been racing since she'd first emerged from Poseidon's waves, unquenched and lustful from her first breath.

Ares fled the dying garden and returned in the company of the entire host of Olympus. Shoulder to shoulder the gods and goddesses formed up around Aphrodite, each one passing awed fingers over the stillness of her chest. Asclepius had brought medicine into the garden, and only he could proclaim what had already been true for centuries: Beauty was dead.

The gods did not understand death. They knew what death was, but only in the sense that they knew what erosion was, what growing old was. It had nothing to do with them.

The gods separated to search for Aphrodite. Hades and Persephone returned to the shores of the roiling Styx and searched for her across the Elysian Fields, and then, with consternation, among the sinners in the bowels of Hell. Hades set Odysseus to calling her name in the long passages that connected the living world and the realm of the dead. Persephone caught her reflection in the pool of Tantalus and was astonished to find a streak of gray nestled into her deep brown hair.

Aphrodite was not in Hell. She was not in Elysia. She was not anywhere. She had ceased.

The notion of nonexistence had never occurred to the gods, and it ignited in them a frenzy that could not be quenched. Zeus refused to believe, and in his disbelief he roamed the world searching for Aphrodite, ravaging the wild shores with the fury of the storm. Demeter tore the earth to pieces to get to Persephone in fear for her daughter, seated so close to the hordes of the dead, and the earth knew no seasons until she had torn her fingernails away. In the shadows of columns that had long since begun to crumble, among marble shards like teeth or broken shells, wise Athena turned her eyes to the stars, which she had counted now and then for practice, always arriving at more or less the same number, and understood for the first time that stars died, and though new ones were born, and the count remained the same, the holes in space stayed empty, the distant songs of old light the only funerary for burnt-out gods.

What was a god who wasn't immortal? Only a man with the power to destroy anything, to live long enough to lose everything he loved. Eternity without beauty was an ugly garden, more thorn than rose. And because she was the only one wise enough to see what was coming, Athena wondered if her death would come like Aphrodite's, a swift supernova, or if gods could also decay, like isotopes, until they were just old stains on the fabric of the world, a worn patch that wanted weaving.

One by one, the old gods caved in, turning their shoulders to the world that was suddenly cold and uncanny, a broken ground too sharp under divine feet.

Hera to the birds, a flare of feathers brilliant as gold in the late light.

Demeter to the trees, the ripple of irate wind in burnished red leaves.

Persephone wasted away to bone, a bored skeleton reposing in Hell's second throne.

Ares surrendered to the sea. His ember limbs hissed in the froth of the waves as he churned in the water, looking for the place Aphrodite first came to be, a tiny cluster of skin cells sloughed off and shining like a pearl under the sand.

Zeus watched them vanish one by one. The thunder unbound him until he was just a spark in a key, a socket, a contact wire in a glass bulb. Out the windows of airplanes, the descendants of demigods perceived the withered carcass of the father: a galaxy of electric lights seeping across the dark face of the sleeping world, calling for the rebirth of Beauty.

Michelle Dotter is the editor-in-chief of *Dzanc Books*, an independent nonprofit publishing house based in Michigan. Her work has appeared in *The Molotov Cocktail, Toasted Cheese, Edify, Crack the Spine,* and the *No Extra Words* podcast. She lives in Boulder, CO.

Wendy J. Fox

The Old Country

In my life then, in high school with my best friend, Cale, I'd say that there was a kind of this layer of not-caring-ness, like in the videos of birds hatching in biology. It's the spot where the chick has started to bust through the shell, but is still encased in the membrane, the grossest part, wet feathers wriggling under a layer of collagen. It's like Cale's face when we used to play bank robbers and we'd stuff our heads into my mom's old pantyhose.

From underneath the nylon, I could sort of see everything and kind of not make out anything, and while the chicks eventually emerge from the egg, it felt like Cale and I were still there, half in and half out, just one tear away from emerging as our full selves, wet and briny and wide-eyed, like if we just reached a little harder, like if there was something more to reach toward.

~~~

Cale and I were in his dad's basement. He had just told me that his dad had said my mom was "smoking hot," and I wasn't sure if I was supposed to pass this information on to my mom or what, so I passed him the bong to try to shut him up.

"I think she's pretty hot too, dude," Cale said, flicking his lighter. He took a long inhale as the water bubbled in the chamber and then he pulled the stem that held the bowl to exhaust the rest of the smoke. "I mean, I guess I hadn't really thought about it until Dad said something and then I was like, *yeah*, totally, *Mrs. D. is a MILF.*"

"Nobody calls my mom Mrs. D.," I said.

"I just did." He passed the bong back.

"She isn't a missus, you know. She's not married. Her name is Linda. You know that," I said.

Cale and I talked a lot, but we didn't talk about the part of what held us together was that both of our parents were divorced. Once in a while, we did things all together, my mom and me with his dad and him, and I think Cale and I both had the same secret hope our parents would fall in love and we would be real brothers. I remember once when the four of us went to a movie, we were sitting in between my mom and his dad, and Cale said something about how we needed to sit on the end, so we moved around until our folks were next to each other. I nodded and he nodded back, but that was as close as we ever got to acknowledging it.

"How old is your mom, anyway," Cale said. "I mean, other than old enough."

"Stop it," I said. We talked like this about women sometimes, but I didn't like it. "I promise you, you are not losing your virginity to my mother."

"Probably true," Cale said. "Hey, give me my lighter."

The two of us didn't really have other friends. We weren't unpopular, we just were gliding through high school, trying to stay invisible. Cale was very good at math, I was very good at English, and we traded our homework around, so we were basically B+ average. I'm sure our teachers knew—we weren't exactly savvy—but like all the other adults around us, there was that gloss of indifference.

~ ~ ~

The thing about my mom was that she gave me this traditional name, Laird, and then she must have thought I'd live up to it. I was all the way in high school before I learned that a laird was someone who owned a large estate. Not Laird, *a* laird. It's like naming your kid Esquire, though it also translates to Lord. I knew other people had this name, but I still always thought it was dumb, though my mom said that she didn't appreciate me being so negative toward her vision for me.

Her *vision* was the way she pronounced it.

It made sense, I guess. We were just on the cusp of girls named Nevaeh—heaven spelled backward, though I wondered, wouldn't the backward of "heaven" be "hell?"—and boys with newly edgy old-timey Bible names like Jedidiah and Zebulon, so Cale and I didn't feel too misplaced. Cale was the Misspelled Vegetable; I was the Lord of Nothing.

My mom and I had the same last name, which was not the same last name as my father.

Also, I don't think we were Scottish—or if we were, we weren't doing anything with it. I mean, we didn't talk about our clans or trace our ancestry or take a trip and call it visiting the "old country." It was rare that we'd go anywhere, but if we did, we'd drive to Arizona or southern California. We went to places that were predictably warm, predictably dry. Usually it was just me and her visiting friends of hers, though once in a while there'd be a boyfriend around.

We didn't really talk about my dad. He'd been gone a long time.

There was one guy, a redhead who, when I was in my earliest teens, started coming around and then he seemed to resurface a lot. For a while I tried to pretend he was my father, even though he was quite a bit younger than my mom, but I had a young mom. She was only twenty when she had me.

I never knew exactly what her *vision* was or what it was supposed to mean, and I didn't ask. She didn't say much about it, except when I complained.

I even thought the redhead and my mom would stay together, but then he hadn't been at our house for a couple of months, and when I mentioned it to Mom, she said she was done with him.

"Why?" I asked. I had liked him, in a way. I had liked him because he seemed like he made her happy mostly, and selfishly, because he was nice to me. I guess I hadn't thought about how he might get in the way of my mom marrying Cale's dad. Sometimes the redhead would slip me a twenty, and the summer that I was fifteen and a half and had my learner's permit, he let me practice driving in his Honda. Which seemed very normal, I thought, a Honda. My mother drove a Grand Am, which might have been a nice car in the nineties sometime, seemed sporty, but now it was trying too hard to hang onto being cool. Kind of like my mom and the redhead.

"He got married, you know," she said. "To his ex. She has some fancy job downtown. We'll see if that lasts," she snorted.

I wasn't sure if my mom meant the job or the marriage, but in any case, it was a long time before I saw the redhead again.

~~~

When Cale and I were juniors in school, we spent most of our time looking for dope. We smoked pot, mostly, because it was the easiest and the cheapest to get, but we preferred acid, mushrooms, or at least that's what we told each other.

"Dude," Cale said after school one Friday, "there's a party at Mark Johnson's house, and I heard there will be 'shrooms."

"I don't have any money," I said.

"No worries," Cale said. "I got you."

Cale's allowance was much larger than mine. Meaning, Cale had an allowance.

There were plenty of single parents in our school, but Cale had the only single dad. To hear him tell it, his mother had run off with some dickbag, a real piece of shit, and even if she wanted to come home, they were not going to let her.

Another thing we didn't talk about was that my dad was that dickbag, that real piece of shit. Cale's actual mom didn't leave with my actual biological dad, just a guy like him. My mom and I, we would have said the same thing about him coming home—that we changed the locks and all that. And we really did.

My mother, kneeling at the door, hardware spread out around her.

Just being smart, my mom had said then.

It was evening, early, but I think I was in pajamas.

We live in a rental house, and you never know how many keys are floating around.

I don't remember so much about him, but I also don't remember nothing. It wasn't dramatic when he left. One day he was there, and the next day he wasn't. I had this cereal bowl with a bear in the bottom of it that I really liked, and sometimes he'd use it for an ashtray. One of the bear's eyes was burned out, but I still ate from it.

I was definitely in pajamas, because I remember the way the footies squished against the vinyl floor.

If your father wants to come inside, he'll need to act right. He's not just barging in. He has to knock.

My mother, her hair pulled back as she worked the old latch and the deadbolt out of its groove, putting the new one in place. She was following the instructions on the package, and I could see her trying very hard to be patient, trying very hard to stay calm.

Later I realized that a lot of people would have called someone, like a locksmith, to come out and do this, or if they were doing it themselves, they would have tools instead of a butter knife as a flathead and a can opener as a wrench.

I was her helper. The face on my bear cereal bowl would keep his other eye.

I was warm in my pajamas.

I held the screws in my outstretched hand.

~~~

There were no mushrooms at Mark Johnson's party. I'm not saying we didn't have fun. Actually, I was a little glad. The only time Cale and I had done mushrooms before, we could only get about half of a very small stem with what was left of his allowance, and so we traded the piece of shrivel back and forth between us, licking it until it was just kind of soggy, like the cardboard that had held an over-used Tootsie Pop.

We swallowed what was left of the stem when it fell apart in my hands.

I'm not sure if we got high, but I know we were tired—we'd stayed up too late, being too careful with the stem.

"Hey, I think I see something," Cale said, just as I was dozing off.

"Is it blue?" I said.

"It's totally blue," he said. "A bright, perfect blue."

"I think that's your dad's bug lamp," I said.

"Right on," Cale said, and his breathing collapsed into snores.

~~~

One thing I remember is that after my mom changed the locks, she was at the peephole all the time, peeking through. She'd hear something and ask me if I heard it, but I couldn't hear anything. Had that been part of her vi*sion*? I wasn't sure.

I was also getting very tired of my pajamas. I wanted to go to school. I wanted to eat my cereal from the bear bowl and brush my teeth and put on my jeans and hop on the bus.

Like Mom *used* to say, "Get out there and hop on the bus, Lairdy."

When I asked about going to school, she said I needed to wait.

"He could be watching," she said.

I didn't think he was watching, and Mom definitely wasn't watching, so I put my cereal in the bear bowl. There was no milk, so I ate it dry. I knew where the washcloths were, so I washed my face and brushed my teeth. I got dressed, and I put my pajamas in the clothes hamper. I took my books from my backpack and spread them on the kitchen table, thinking of my teacher and my desk.

"What are you doing?" she asked.

"School," I said. I still had dry cereal stuck in my teeth, and I was working it out with my tongue.

"I'm so proud of you, Laird," she said.

"Thank you," I said. One piece of Cheerio came loose.

I wanted to tell her I didn't know where to start in my workbook, but she was already back at the peephole.

~~~

The thing about my mom was that she was okay, eventually. One day I woke up and she had my lunch pail and clean pants and she was rushing me out the door, and it was *Hop on the bus, Lairdy!* again.

I was nervous about showing up, but it turns out missing three weeks of the second grade is not the worst thing. Mom went back to work. The peephole stayed undarkened. We didn't talk about it.

Years later, when the redhead left, I asked if we were going to change the locks, and she said, *Laird? Wait, what? Um, no.*

~~~

In fact, I wasn't sure what my mother's *vision* was at all, for herself, or for me. We stayed in the same house; she worked the same job. I hung out with Cale; she hung out with ladies from her office—she was an administrative assistant, and even now I correct someone who says "secretary." *Show a little respect*, I'll say. *Unless you are talking about the Secretary of State or something, it's* administrative assistant, *seriously*.

I think my mom would have really liked to have a daughter. The one time I took a girl to a dance, she asked if Brianna could come over beforehand.

"Maybe I could do her makeup?"

"I don't think so, Mom. That's weird."

But I guess I was wrong because when I told Bri about it later, when I was trying to help her understand that I didn't get weird all on my own, Bri said she thought it was sweet. She said, *Hey, have your mom call me anytime. I would totally get a pedi with her*, but I didn't tell my mom anything about that.

It's not like Bri ever called me after that one dance, so it was definitely not like I was going to set her up with my mom.

~~~

"Guys, I need you to keep the windows open down there if you are going to be smoking in the basement," Cale's dad said. "I really don't care, but be a little more conscientious, you know?"

Once, Cale's dad had told me to call him by his first name, Kevin, but I didn't want to call him Kevin.

"Yeah, but we're not really *smoking*, Dad," Cale said.

"No? Then why does the basement smell like a skunk? Enlighten me."

"It's more like, I mean, not to put too fine a point, but technically we're more like taking massive bong rips," Cale said.

"That involves smoke," his dad said, "that you inhale into your lungs and then exhale, which is smoking. Technically."

"Whatever, man, you're the engineer," said Cale.

It was true. Cale's dad was an engineer. He was kind of a dork, but I understood how that could be cool once you weren't in high school anymore. Like Cale's dad wouldn't even need to call a locksmith because he had his own tools. Cale's dad probably knew how to make a key from a wax mold or whatever professional lock people did.

"What do you think, Laird? Smoking or not smoking?"

This was supposed to be the place where I could shine and use a word like *nomenclature* or *colloquialism*. Instead, I made a dumb kind of pun and I said, "All I know is I heard you think my mom is *smoking* hot."

Cale wouldn't meet my eyes, but his dad lifted an eyebrow.

"Back to the basement, guys. Keep the window open."

For the rest of the afternoon, we watched TV in the quiet.

~~~

When we were seniors, Cale got a scholarship, because he was the one who was good at math. Our final year was horrible in that same pantyhose on the head way. We'd try to hang out and have fun, but I knew he was moving and I was going to stay home and go to the community college, and every moment was punctured by the idea of him leaving.

Cale's dad said it didn't matter where anyone went, it only mattered what you did.

"You can still come over any time, buddy," he said to me.

On the day Cale left for the dorms, I helped him load his stuff into the car and I kept wondering if I should tell him that I loved him, because I did really love him, but when he went to get in the passenger side, his dad already belted in, I didn't have words.

"Peace, dude," Cale said.

"Peace," I said.

We didn't hug or even shake hands or chest bump, not that we had ever chest bumped.

As the car pulled away from the house, I kept wondering what that sound was, *what was that horrible snorting sound*, until my mom pulled me in close to her and I realized it was me, crying and sniveling and really kind of freaking out.

"Oh, Lairdy Laird," she said. "I'm so sorry. This was not in the *vision*."

~~~

While Cale was at school, sometimes he and I would email, in a sentimental way.

Dear Lord of Nothing, he would write.

Hello, Misspelled Vegetable! I'd respond.

Once in a while, when he was back home for the holidays, we'd smoke pot in his dad's basement and we'd open the window, we'd be conscientious.

Cale talked about his classes—advanced geometry and trig. His lab partner in organic chem was a real shit, I learned.

"What are the girls like in junior college?" he asked.

"What did you say?" I hated that, *junior college*.

"At your school, what are the girls like."

"They're girls. I mean, not really girls. There are a lot of returning students, which is cool, in the mix." I hoped I sounded like I knew what I was talking about.

"So, they're easy?" Cale pulled the stem out of the bong, in the same way he always had.

"What?"

"Nothing, dude. It's just... Sorority chicks. You are missing out."

~ ~ ~

I actually really loved my community college. The instructors were kind. My peers had lives and homes, and some had kids of their own, and we were all working pretty hard. Cale had told me about massive lecture halls with hundreds of students, and I wasn't sure how that was better than a small classroom.

I did eventually transfer to a university, downtown, at the extension campus. By that time, Cale was already starting to think about PhD programs, and I was still living with my mom.

It will mostly come down to where I get funding, he said over email.

I wasn't sure what to say. I knew it wasn't cool to be a twenty-something guy and not have my own place, and I was taking creative writing classes, so I definitely was getting a more sophisticated understanding of cliché.

Of course I wasn't planning on staying in my childhood room forever, but I liked being up early in our house. I'd go for a run in the filmy dawn and then make coffee for both of us. My mom had always used cheap grounds in an electric percolator, but I ground beans and heated water for French press, and when it was just ready to pour, I tapped at her room. She'd come out, in her robe, and we'd have the coffee, and I'd poach eggs and make toast. A guy at school I hung out with sometimes had taught me about coffee, and the same guy had showed me how to make eggs.

I had tried to write about the mornings with my mom in my creative writing workshop, and I had tried again to write about it in an email to Cale, and both said it was some kind of Oedipal thing. I couldn't get on the page how it wasn't—it was more of a shift, a tear in the nylon, getting to know my mom as an adult.

I mean, she was my mother and I was her son, and we had a lot of hard times after my dad left when she was scared and I was too young to do anything or even know how to do anything, and now that I was old enough, I just wanted to make my mother a nice cup of fucking coffee and be kind to her because I was still working on how to say, *Hey, thank you for holding it together; that must have been really hard, I can't even imagine,* and the only way sometimes is to do some other kindness like the coffee and a perfect egg on perfect toast, and it doesn't take away what it would feel like to have an eyeball glued to the peephole for three terrified weeks, but it is something. It was all I had to give, and I wanted to give it to her, every single day.

When Cale emailed, less and less, and he asked how my mom was, I wanted to say, *Dude, what are you doing for your dad? People get lonely, you know.* But I didn't.

In early summer, just before I graduated, I invited Cale's dad over for dinner. Maybe it was a last ditch of trying to hold the connection with Cale, our old fantasy of our folks falling in love.

We had a good time. I made a roast and Kevin brought wine and we drank our way through a couple of bottles, but it was clear there was nothing between my mom and him, never had been, besides me and Cale.

The dinner was a kind of ending, and I wished my friend was there to see it.

~~~

Cale got his funding for a doctoral program, and I got a job in an office. I still wanted to write, but I knew it wouldn't pay. I started as a temp and then was hired full time. I had my own apartment then, and there were things I liked about it, but there were also times it seemed ridiculous, when I'd be sitting around by myself and my mom was sitting around by herself and we were probably both wondering what the point of separation was while we stared at the wall.

At my office holiday party, that first year, I was talking to my coworkers Heather, Sabine, and Michael, and I saw a flash of red hair.

"Who is that?"

"James," Sabine said. "Heidi's husband."

Heidi was our boss, but my mom and I had always called her husband, before he was my boss's husband, when he drove a Honda and slipped me twenties, Jimmy, sometimes Jaime.

We were standing by the makeshift bar, a low table that had been set up near the copy machine.

"They're still together?" I asked.

"Barely," said Heather, taking a long pull of her drink. "At least to hear Heidi tell it. I don't know. I try not to ask too much."

I wasn't sure then what to do, but I did start to understand my mother's *vision*. You have even a slightly unusual name and people won't forget it—he might have forgotten my face, and my face had changed in any case, but how many vaguely familiar guys named *Laird* could he really know.

"Hey, Heather, introduce me?"

~~~

We went outside so Jimmy could smoke. He said he was supposed to be quitting, but he was always looking for excuses. Like seeing someone from the past, he said as he lit up, that was a good enough excuse.

There was a light snow, but it wasn't too cold. There was a pretty glow of holiday lights as we ducked under an awning.

"Who was that kid you were always so obsessed with," Jimmy said. "I always thought he was a punk, but Linda asked me not to say anything."

"Cale," I said. "He's doing a PhD in theoretical mathematics."

"And your mother?"

"She's well," I said. "But bored, I think."

"We're all bored," Jimmy said, smoke puffing out of his last syllable. "I missed her, you know, and I missed you."

I wasn't sure what to say. We looked around, as red and green flashed on the white snow.

"I guess I didn't think I'd ever see you again," I said.

He nodded. When I blinked against the snow, it could have just as easily been Cale there, kicking at the ice near the curb.

"So, I think this is good," I said.

Jimmy stamped out his cigarette.

The wind had shifted to feel like a bite, and I turned my collar up.

I knew I would tell my mother I'd seen him, and I was already thinking what I'd say.

He didn't look good, you know, like not bad or unhealthy, just…not happy.

I knew it, she'd say. *I knew it.*

And we would be having this conversation in the morning because I would have gotten up early enough to make it to my mom's place in time to make the coffee. I would have sent a text to Cale that he would probably never return, and on Monday I would go to work and see my boss, who was screwing my mom's old boyfriend.

When the snow started swirling harder, Jimmy had gone back to the office party, and when I blinked I saw the bear with the missing eye, cereal falling into the bowl.

Lord of Nothing.

Her vi*sion*.

One perfect egg, on perfect toast.

Wendy J. Fox is the author of "The Seven Stages of Anger and Other Stories", the novel "The Pull of It" and the forthcoming novel "If the Ice Had Held." She has also been published widely in literary magazines and journals.

Madeline Anthes

When I Learned a Certain Power

I broke boys' hearts in my parents' driveway. It was always late, long after my parents went to sleep.

I walked outside barefoot. These boys always waited, hands in pockets, knowing it was coming.

Of course it was.

Summer nights ran a current through me. My feet were warm on sun-drunk tar, and I watched their heads droop.

As they retreated back to their cars, I almost willed them back. Pulled them in again. Rolled them in my hands to squeeze them in my fist. To feel them break.

But I let them go. Another would come soon.

I smiled.

Madeline Anthes is the acquisitions editor for *Hypertrophic Literary*. Her writing can be found in journals like *WhiskeyPaper*, *Lost Balloon*, *Cease*, *Cows*, and *Third Point Press*. You can find her on Twitter at @maddieanthes.

Stephen C. Middleton

By Choice?

Keloid scars

Art after Hiroshima

A scar after surgery

Mirrored by the photograph

But *this* scar was caused

By a machete

In the Congo

Or simple sleep deprivation

& pain

For which *I* was medicated

Here gleeful inflicted

Unspeakable

Or; with cystoscopy,

Unanaeathetised laminectomy

I would talk

Spill reams

& the chill walk to

Operating theatre

The chill walk to

Torture chamber or

The scaffold

Whatever

It is, after all,

Only a little neck.

Stephen C. Middleton is a writer working in London, England. He has had five books published, including "A Brave Light" (*Stride*) and "Worlds of Pain / Shades of Grace" (*Poetry Salzburg*). He has been in several anthologies, among them "Paging Doctor Jazz" (*Shoestring*), "From Hepworth's Garden Out" (*Shearsman*, 2010), and "Yesterday's Music Today" (*Knives Forks And Spoons*, 2015). For many years he was editor of *Ostinato*, a magazine of jazz and jazz inspired poetry, and *The Tenormen Press*. He has been in many magazines worldwide. Current projects (prose and poetry) relate to jazz, blues, politics, outsider (folk) art, mountain environments, and long-term illness.

Joe Ponepinto

Ungrounded

Perhaps he had forgotten to turn the power off to work on the wiring. But even house current can knock you on your ass. An electrician would never dismiss the basics of the trade.

It's just a tingle, he said, once you get used to it. Sometimes my fingers go numb for a minute, but it's nothing.

There must have been a first time, a jolt that kicked the tool from his hand, surged up his arm and into his brain and welded him, for a second, to a vision of his demise. He must have sat there, afterward, licking the burn on his fingertips and cursing his stupidity.

As he worked he talked: baseball, politics, God, science; talked so incessantly that I couldn't break from his monologue long enough to leave the room. His car, his wife, the weather, his vacation in the woods. He had a story for everything, and told them all, as though incapable of stopping himself. And so I kept him company, watching his fingers dash among the wires: the red, the black, the yellow and white twisted pair, their copper tongues flicking like snakes' as they fired electrons into his flesh. Every few seconds he jerked and let them go, and then shook his head and dove back in for more. The green wire, I noticed, he kept separate, one end screwed to a metal plate, the other limp in the air.

I expected him to tell me he was lucky to be alive, to launch into a sermon on divine intervention and how I should let Jesus into my life. Or to tell me of a secret dream he had about standing on a cliff in a thunderstorm and raising his lightning rod into the air. Instead he went on about the quotidian, emptying his fried green tomato of a brain as he built up immunity, I suppose, to the electric chair.

Had he been already rendered senseless when he next stared at live wires and decided it wasn't worth the effort to go downstairs and open the breakers? The sober conscience recoils from memories of pain, but his did not.

In the early days of current patients danced like marionettes in hospital hallways, the heavy leads taped to their bodies in an effort to torture psychoses away. They begged the doctors to spare them, but many would lose their minds in the cause of science.

When he patched up the wall and declared the house functional again, the electrician extended his hand. I took it in mine and refused to let go. He struggled, handcuffed in my grip, complaining that he had other houses, other clients to visit. But I held on, my hand squeezing his like vise grips, and looked for something made of metal that I could grasp with the other.

Joe Ponepinto's novel, "Mr. Neutron," was published by *7.13 Books* in March, 2018. He was the founding publisher and fiction editor of *Tahoma Literary Review*. He has had stories published in *Crab Orchard Review, Fugue, Lumina*, and dozens of other literary journals in the U.S. and abroad. A New Yorker by birth, he has lived in many places around the country, and now resides in Washington State with his wife, Dona. He is an adjunct writing instructor at Seattle's Hugo House and Tacoma Community College.

Jessica B. Weisenfels

A Triptych in Trees

I. Judah

I saw Alex's mother at the grocery store and she invited me to coffee the next day at the Starbucks in Burnstown. She's old now, pushing seventy and still in a tie dye broomstick skirt I recognized from back when I was a teen. She's a little less bright than she used to be, but still shiny. Like a hall mirror going darker with dirt and time. I feel myself getting that way too, older and further away from the people I used to be. As I dressed to meet her I felt the shame of choices I didn't make creep up my throat.

"If anyone would have told me that between the two of you, he'd be the one to marry a good man and move to Bentonville to work for the Waltons, I'd've called bullshit."

I stirred my coffee and nodded into the cup.

"I always thought it would be you to choose that kind of life, but I'm glad for what you did choose. You look well, and I know you're a good mama." She hunched her shoulders, leaned in across the small table, "You know post-divorce is a good time to go get yours. Anybody from your past popping up yet?"

I smiled at her, told her about the all the old flames who sent me messages on social media. Then she asked the question I didn't want to hear. Three words and the weight of them like an anvil coming right down on me.

"What about Judah?"

I shook my head and changed the subject. She said it in an even tone, threw it away like it was nothing, but when I climbed in bed that night, it was waiting for me. I whispered it to the low, white ceiling above my bed, shifting the emphasis of the cool, round syllables. What *about* Judah, then *what* about Judah, then what about *Judah*.

If I'm honest, I spent a good portion of my marriage thinking about him. I made a choice one too-hot September afternoon under a grove of pecan trees, and I spent all this time wondering if it was wrong. My boyfriend, now my ex-husband, was playing a gig with his band over in the Burnstown city square that night. We were eighteen and about to be engaged. It was before I understood what it meant to be someone's wife.

Judah appeared like magic, leaner and taller than I remembered. He hated town events, called them Parades of Hypocrisy. I was surprised to see him. It had been a little over a year since he'd shattered me with our breakup. He'd been the model boyfriend. A boy wonder math genius two years younger than I was. Tall and angular with hair like haystacks. Feline jawbone and steady green eyes flecked with gold making him more like a lion than a boy. Romantic and devoted in ways I still struggle to understand, but a fan of pills and marijuana too. The pills and weed built the mystique of him, and everyone gave him sidelong glances over it.

I had a bit of a reputation of my own back in the day. I was among the smartest in my class, a model citizen at school, president of five clubs my senior year. But from the time I was fourteen my after-school activities included various kinds of sex mostly with partners far too old for me, and it's hard to keep a double life secret in a town of three thousand. Dedham is the death of secrets.

I never dated boys my own age, partly because they found me intimidating and partly out of a desire to protect their innocence. I had a wildness and hunger that I didn't want to infect them with. A near-constant desire to have hot flesh pushed up against me. I especially did not date anyone younger than myself.

Judah was different. He was the most extraordinary person I'd ever met. Creative and brilliant and odd enough to be the same kind of outsider I was. He became my best friend quickly, and the best boyfriend I ever had shortly after that. People said, "Y'all are soulmates."

I didn't believe in soulmates. Still don't. But I thought twice about it over the eight months we were together.

When he broke my heart, I spent weeks crying into Alex's shoulder, sitting at Alex's mother's kitchen table crying some more. Alex knew what the breakup was over, but I made a lie to offer everyone else. Judah broke my heart because I took his virginity. Though he loved substances, religious shame from a troubled childhood seeped in when it came to pleasures of the flesh. He told me he didn't need another demon. Judah left me lonely, ashamed of things I'd never been ashamed of before. Back then I never thought about how lonely Alex must have been, the only young gay man in the whole town. In some ways that pulse of loneliness in our teen years drew us deeper into a friendship that had already spanned most of our lives. We spent a lot of time being lonely together. Then one day I finally cried Judah out of my system, or that's what I thought in the moment, anyway. I picked myself up, had a few one-night stands, fell into a real relationship with a greasy twenty-six-year-old vegan punk rocker, and graduated from high school.

I met Harold six months into that relationship. He walked into our freshman level history class with deep brown curls under an orange bandana that had tiny yellow flowers on it. I wanted him, so I took him. Mr. 26-year-old Vegan Punk Rocker was unceremoniously dumped and Harold, Alex, and I moved my stuff out of the tiny apartment we had shared in the middle of the night while he was heading back from a Weezer show in Missouri.

Back then I swore Harold was Judah's opposite: shorter, bearded, stocky, face surrounded by browns in place of Judah's golden hues. Unbelievable musician, but terrible at math. Harold grew from an average middle-class family, the kind of family who reveres the generations their people held plantations, while Judah lived in government housing with his former-sexpot mom. Harold's half-hearted Catholicism to Judah's unhinged backwoods nondenominational Christianity. See? I said to myself, They're nothing alike.

But when Harold and I were together, people said, "Y'all are soulmates," and deep down I knew everything I loved about him was separated by a thin filament from everything I'd loved about Judah. They were not opposites, but mirrors. I told myself I just had a type, but I wondered if that type had come to be because I'd loved Judah. Did I ever really believe Harold was my soulmate? Well, no. Of course not. At least that's how I see it now.

Under the pecan trees that day, Judah told me he'd heard I worked at the coffee shop in Fort Smith and he'd hoped to catch me there. Another boy from our town had already told me that, but I nodded like I didn't know, said I was sorry I'd missed him. His green eyes focused on mine, made me feel whole the way they had the year before, and I could not walk away. I wanted to, but I couldn't.

"How's school?" he asked.

"I'm thinking of dropping out. I can't decide what I want to do."

"That would be incredibly stupid."

"You don't get to say that to me," I shot back at him.

"I'm sorry. I just meant you're too smart—you should have gone off somewhere to school . MIT like we—you always planned."

"I've got siblings to look after. I can't do that from Massachusetts," I turned to walk away.

"Marianne, I was hoping to tell you . . ." he paused, and I turned to face him.

"It's okay. We're cool. Everything worked out for the best," I told him.

He smiled sadly and took a deep breath, "I wanted to tell you that you deserve everything. You deserve everything that makes you happy. . ." he paused then, and I felt my face go red. "I—no…" He looked at the ground too late. I had already seen on his face what he meant. "You deserve to have everything you want. I've been waiting months to tell you that. Half a year."

In that moment I knew I could walk to him and tell him that I wanted him. I could make the choice to have him again. But Harold arrived before I could speak, his deep brow set in a scowl.

In the car on the way home, Harold was more jealous than anyone I'd ever encountered, and he was mean about it too. I was still young enough to think that was romantic. Though we'd only been together a few months, he proposed the next day and I accepted. Looking back, I think he never would have done it if I hadn't gone off to talk to Judah.

It was like Judah's shadow slid into the car on that hot September night, and it followed us. It followed when we married a few months later. It lurked in the hallway of our first small apartment. It stood in the bathroom doorway when I had my first miscarriage. It was with me when I dropped out of college because my young marriage was already falling apart. It followed us when we brought our baby boy home from the hospital the year after that. Anniversaries, birthdays, holidays, I thought of Judah. I wrapped my legs around my husband and thought of Judah. For a decade.

Harold had his own shadows. A girl named April, rum, and a sadness that clung to him like a grease stain.

The affair that ended my marriage was mine, with a man I met when I went back to school in my late twenties. It lasted several months and I didn't even like him. But he had hair like haystacks and it was close enough to the real thing. The worst part is that Harold had gotten over that initial jealousy. After our second child was born he complained about the weight the pregnancies had put on me, but he never got jealous again. I'm not saying he was a good husband. He never kept steady work. He never took care of the boys. But the hardest truth is this: I was bored with my life, so I had an affair.

Even now, five years after our divorce, I think I should have chosen Judah under those trees. Judah who cared if I graduated from college. Judah who thought I should have what I wanted.

Seventeen years apart from that evening under the trees, and one small chain of events stands at the center of my life. Almost exactly the median of my days, between my birth and these thirty-four years I've lived so far. It starts with the moment when Judah showed up after the fall formal in jeans and a tee shirt, waiting at the huge double doors for me to come out. Rain pouring little rivers down his face. A memory in dreary tones, the dark soft focus of a youth I lost too soon. He said, "I was bored. I came to see if you wanted to go back to my house and talk." My date that night was my best friend Alex. He kissed my cheek and told me to go. I remember how those who didn't know us thought it was odd that Alex let me go. People thought he was probably gay, but it wasn't until that chaste kiss that anyone was sure. The grass was a thin sheet over inches of mud made by those torrential autumn storms, and when I took Judah's hand to step out onto it, my heels sunk. Something ridiculous happened then. Something out of a movie, a scene that I'd roll my eyes at now. Judah, who towered over me but probably weighed less than my tall, muscular body allowed, leaned down and picked me up. He carried me to my truck, in the rain, with Alex and the rest of the high school seniors of Dedham High clapping in the background. He set me down and whispered, "Should we give them more to talk about?" I pulled back and threw him against the driver's side door, kissing him like I'd kissed a hundred men, but making him feel like he was the only one.

When I pull these things apart, when I look under the skin of my ten-year failure, I see those romantic moments that continued to flicker across the back of my mind. And now, at thirty-four, I think of how much life I wasted waiting on anything that compared.

I never forgot, not for a moment, that Judah broke up with me because we slept together after months and months of foreplay. He thought demons came into him that night. I always wondered why sex demons were worse than the ones already crawling all over him.

When I went to Alex's mother to tell her I was engaged to Harold, she was surprised. I was surprised when it wasn't because of my age. But then again, most Dedham girls were married by twenty.

"You know I love Mr. Douglas. He's my best friend and a great husband. I mean that. But Marianne, when I was young I loved another man," she twisted her hand in her long paisley skirt and then turned her eyes back to me, "If that man came to my door and asked me to run away with him, I'm not absolutely sure that I wouldn't pack my bags and go. I don't want that to happen to you. I think Judah might be that man for you someday, honey, but if you say you love this new Harold like you loved Judah, I'll believe you."

"I'm really happy, Mrs. Douglas. Believe me," I smiled my best smile, the one I think means I'm not lying.

"Just be careful you don't have your soul tied up somewhere else."

I came to wonder if she was right, if I did have my soul tied up somewhere else. I had dreams about it. Judah showing up in the doorway of the three-bedroom brick house we owned when I was still married. It was always raining in the dream, and Judah never said anything. He just held out his hand, and I never hesitated. I took his hand and we disappeared. Faded into the rain like fog.

I still wonder if it wasn't the shadow of some great love that followed me all those years, but instead the fleeing of little bits of my soul on their way to find all we'd lost. Sometimes it does feel like a part of me has gotten smaller, stretched thin by the dissonance between what I wanted and what I chose. Some days it feels like Judah could whisper my name from halfway across the world and I'd hear it. Most days it seems like Judah was a movie I never stayed to finish. A goodness I could never keep. A want that still burns inside me.

II. All They'd Lost

She was with her children when she saw him again. There he was, in the corner booth of the Dedham Whole Hawg, eating much like any stranger or polite acquaintance would. In total ignorance of her presence there. In her weaker moments, she thought if they met again there'd be a current in the room. Not enough to lift her feet from the grass like before, but enough that he'd lift his still-blond head and know, somehow, that she was standing there. The defining moment in the movie she never finished. The moment when everything changes.

She looked at her sons. Teddy was dutifully staring at his phone, as fourteen-year-olds were wont to do. Tyler, fresh from his eighth birthday, was admiring the cinnamon rolls in the case. Judah sat in the corner booth, even thinner than he'd been all those years ago. Too thin. Long face a mask set above sinewy long neck over collarbone jutting out like a small bluff. He was refugee camp thin. Gaunt eyes looking out from a history book. Meth thin. Another good boy lost in the sea of skeletons.

Someone said he'd been out in the Oklahoma panhandle, but she hadn't heard he'd come back to the county. She paid for the two pies she'd ordered, slipped out the door with her sons, and headed over to her grandmother's house for the family dinner. She found her sister leaned against the storage building, smoking a cigarette and watching her niece jump on the trampoline.

"Can I have one?"

"Thought you quit," Tessa replied, handing her the pack.

"Did you know Judah was back in town?" Marianne asked.

"Judah Moore?"

"Yeah, dumbass, Judah Moore."

"Of course I did, why?"

Marianne looked at the ground, wishing she'd dropped off the boys and called Alex instead. Tessa's wide brown eyes grew huge in her face.

"Oh shit. Y'all used to date, huh?"

116

"Yeah," she said, thinking that the word wasn't enough. Date. It sounded so small.

"Well, you'll see him Sunday at Aurora's birthday party."

"Why the fuck did you invite him to Aurora's birthday party?"

"Oh shit. You're really upset."

"No, I'm fine. Sorry," Marianne took a deep drag of her cigarette and broke into a coughing fit.

Tessa patted her back, "Slow down, slick. I didn't realize it meant that much to you."

"I didn't either." It might not have been the truth, but Marianne's little sister was a heart-breaking badass, a woman who left a wake of a thousand shattered men, and she didn't want to lose face or weep before the pie was served.

"You might need to sit down for this next part," Tessa said.

Marianne nodded, but didn't sit.

"You remember Ryan's mom, Aggie?"

Ryan was Aurora's father, a beautiful country boy who turned out to have a pretty intense drug selling habit. His mother was worse. Marianne nodded.

"Judah has been back for two years. Living with Aggie."

Marianne let the information wash over her. It nearly swept her off her feet. Aggie was so old. Old enough to be Judah's mother.

From the trampoline, Aurora began wailing. Tessa walked away, called over her shoulder, "You better get your shit together, sis. Your niece calls him Papa Judah now."

Marianne finished her cigarette, thinking of the boy with hair like haystacks.

On Sunday Marianne wore her best dress, the kind of garden party dress that looked even better with a petticoat. The dress was a deep plum that complimented her dark eyes, the same color she'd worn on the first night she'd kissed Judah. She swept the same shade over her eyelids and glazed her lips in a pale pink. She twisted her hair into a knot, took it down, braided it, and arrived with it flowing around her shoulders.

Teddy went off to sit on a bench away from his young cousins, and Tyler laid their gift for Aurora on a picnic table and went off to swing with the birthday girl. Marianne scanned the park for Aggie and Judah, but they had not arrived. She helped Tessa with the decorations, carefully taping down the plastic tablecloth and setting the water bottles in perfectly straight lines. After it was all done, she asked Tessa for another cigarette. Tessa obliged, but rolled her eyes. Marianne decided to buy a pack on the way home.

Aggie and Judah arrived, Judah's arm wrapped around her waist. They approached the table, their gift for Aurora in a grocery store sack twisting around Judah's finger. Aggie hugged Tessa, Tessa's thick, strong arms obscuring the bones in Aggie's back, which showed through the cut out in her thin shirt. Judah locked eyes with Marianne and nodded in greeting. A thrill went down her spine. His flesh may have gone down to bone and aged beyond his years, but those steady green eyes were still exactly the same. Here he was, her boy, a grown man in a tattered, oversized tee shirt. Standing, again, under treetops.

Tessa hugged Judah next, and Marianne greeted Aggie, somehow jealous of the touch her sister was receiving. When Aggie wandered off to find her granddaughter, Judah stayed.

Tessa suddenly made herself busy transporting presents to a picnic table halfway across the small park, and Marianne was alone with Judah.

"So . . ." she began.

"Heard you've done well . . ." Judah spoke over her.

Instead of giggling like they might have when they were younger, they both looked at the ground. Marianne's face went bright red.

"You want some water?" Marianne asked to cover her embarrassment.

"I can reach the water," Judah smiled, the stretch of his skin wrinkling beyond his age in that posture.

"So . . . what are you up to these days?" Marianne asked.

"Oh, this and that. I hear you're the branch manager over at the bank."

"I am," Marianne replied.

"And you got two boys."

Marianne nodded. "I'm sorry, I don't really know what you've been up to. I didn't even know you were back in town until…"

"Until you went to pick up the pies the other day."

Marianne gaped.

"I saw you. I didn't know if you'd want to talk to me, so I didn't want to make it all awkward in front of your boys."

"You saw me?"

Judah leaned in, collapsing the world around them until Tessa's loud laughter from ten feet away seemed to disappear. Marianne nearly gasped when he smelled like he always had—marijuana and Old Spice.

"I'll always see you. I can still feel it when you're in the room."

Marianne's face flushed again.

Aggie approached then, wrapping her arm around Judah's waist.

"You two catching up?" Aggie asked, good-naturedly.

Judah nodded, "It's been a long time. I was just asking if my old friend got everything she ever wanted."

Marianne smiled her best smile for Aggie, "I told him no one gets everything they wanted."

"Girl, ain't that the truth. We can get pretty close, though, cain't we?" Aggie stood on her tiptoes and planted a kiss on Judah's cheek. He stared through Marianne as she did it.

Marianne did buy a pack of cigarettes on her way home. She smoked five after her boys went to bed, sitting on her front porch among the herbs, thinking about how sad Judah's life had become. She hoped he'd turn it around. She hoped he was happy. She hoped he'd move back to the panhandle and she'd never have to see him again. When her phone rang at two a.m., she answered even though she didn't know the number.

"I'm sorry. I thought you would be asleep. Same number since high school, huh?"

Marianne drew a deep breath. "You remembered my number?"

"I remember all your numbers," Judah said. "Anyway, I didn't mean to wake you. I was going to leave a voicemail, see if you wanted to grab a coffee sometime?"

Marianne let the silence hang for a moment, imagined walking into the Burnstown Starbucks with Judah, her bright boy who always smelled of marijuana and Old Spice. His face. His beautiful face. The image changed before her, hair like haystacks over that obvious skull. A ratty shirt with a junk store jacket thrown over it, dirty jeans too big for his too-thin frame. She let out a sigh.

"This silence feels like a death, Marianne." His voice pulled back the image and she wanted to say yes so badly she could feel it burning her throat.

There was temptation there, to clean him up. To save him. But the image came back when he didn't speak, and the thought of being in public with him . . . people would think he was homeless. He wore a hard life stretched in his skin, and she couldn't stop seeing the ruin. And there was something deeper, too. Could she afford to sink her whole big life into his salvation?

"I'm sorry, Judah. I can't."

"Alright, I knew it was a long shot."

"I just—I can't. I'm so sorry. I have to go. Work tomorrow."

"Okay." She remembered the way he went still when he couldn't face something. The night he broke her heart, that stillness she couldn't stand. He was so animated, so much a fidgeting energy, but she felt him go still across the line.

"It was really good to see you again, Judah. I mean that. You have a good night, okay?"

"Marianne—wait . . ."

She waited, though the quiet stretched a beat too long.

"Did . . . I mean, I know you didn't get everything you wanted, but are you happy? Are you happy in your life?"

She did not hesitate. "No, I'm not."

"Are you at least satisfied?" She remembered him in a copse of trees that seemed a life apart. Judah saying she should have what she wanted.

"Mostly." She smiled then, smiled at that telling of a hard-won truth, and said her goodbyes.

When she finally fell back asleep she dreamt him standing at her front door, a dream just like the one she had had a million times before, this time with a change to the ending. Instead of taking his hand, she looked into his steady eyes and watched as he disappeared into the rain like fog. He never said a word in the dream, and by Aurora's next birthday, he was dead.

III. Mathematics

When I think of her I think of dimensions. I used to keep her senior picture hidden in my wallet. I marked it up to figure her ratios so I could memorize her in digits.

Approximately 1.62. The number as elemental human need. Top of head to pupil. Width of nose. Nosetip to chin. The golden ratio of attraction. Her face is nearly ideal. The nose is slightly too wide, but her eyes are mathematically perfect. When I dream her, I see her face in equations, her laughter in visible rounds of spiral. Up and up it winds and into trees and running through the spirals of leaves and their little breathing mouths. Spiral on spiral on perfect golden ratio, macro- and microcosm of her and us and feeding into itself. Into ourselves. When she speaks it's the number. "1.61803398875," she says. Forever and ever in the dream. Her lips twisting a half-smile as she says it. I carry her through the rain a hundred years a night and she never says anything but the number. The number over and over again and never my name. The number and a spinning laugh dancing on treetops.

When I met her husband I wondered if he dreamt her in sounds. I know people who know him now. He's the best blues guitarist in the county, they say. I wonder where he puts her mouth on the fret board, what lonely sound the bridge of her nose makes.

I memorized pi to the one hundred and seventy fifth digit when I knew her best. Thought it was the perfect number. I still think it sometimes. Smoke up. Write it out on the walls in chalk. Aggie wipes it off. I feel the loss then, a burning ache like she's dead. It stings my eyes. I ask Aggie why she did that and she says I'm too crazy about numbers and asks why I don't pay more attention to our life together.

After the park I write her on the wall in numbers, in marker this time. Close my eyes and see her face in living color. Remember her in centimeters. The only portrait I can make. 1.76 for her nose and the span of her face. 1.67 for lips to chin. Innerocular distance as compared to width of eyes, 1.61803398875.

Jessica B. Weisenfels lives in the Arkansas Ozarks, where she accumulates chronic diseases and steals language from her children. Her poetry can be found in *Fence, E-ratio,* Sink Review, and a few other places. Her fiction has been published by *Fiction Southeast, Crack the Spine, the Yalobusha Review,* and *Apt.*

Jessamine Price

Forward

I'm competitive about grief. It catches me by surprise, whenever I hear about a suicide. A voice in my head says, I can beat that. I think nicer things, too—how terrible, what a shame—but the selfish, caveman part of me is sure that Cindy's suicide was worse. My oldest friend Cindy appeared happy and successful—until the day she wrote a note and poisoned herself.

How strong I am for bearing it, how well-adjusted. Look at how I just keep moving forward.

In our third-grade classroom, she hunched around in a home-knit sweater, trying to hide that she was the tallest girl in the class. I was a small kid myself, and I thought she was strange. But she liked poetry, so we were friends.

By high school, she stood straighter, but I noticed another kind of awkwardness. Walking down the street or at the mall, she was unable to walk in a straight line. When we walked side-by-side, she leaned to one side slightly. She would crowd and trip me. Then after wandering into my path, she would wander away again. Soon she would be at arm's length, her eyes on the horizon ahead as if she was walking alone.

Her pace was odd too. She would slow down or speed up with no regard to the person next to her. I felt ignored.

I thought she was trying to drive me nuts. One time I elbowed her in the side. Another time I stopped walking completely and stood on the sidewalk sulking. She didn't notice, she just kept moving forward.

But I learned how to walk next to her, in our twenty-seven years of friendship. I adjusted my pace so no one would think she was weird—this woman in the well-tailored suit who couldn't quite fit in, who tipped a bit to one side and was always looking at something in the distance.

I asked her finally, when we were adults. Did she know she had trouble walking in a straight line? She looked surprised. She hadn't noticed.

Hm, she said, I wonder why.

I suspected something neurological. Walking in a straight line takes high-level skills in perception and balance. Was she missing something? How did her strange gait connect to her strange decision to leave behind friends, family, and a good career to end her life?

We buried Cindy's mysteries with her, on a cold day in early October. In the church hall where we gathered after the service, there was a photo that her sister took.

She is small and distant, a dark figure in a dark jacket walking on a wide gray beach under a cloudy sky.

She was in her own little world, her sister said. She fell so far behind, I turned and took a photo of her in the distance. I don't know if she noticed.

Why does she still move forward?

Jessamine has an MFA in creative writing from American University, where she was the prose editor of *Folio*. She also has an M.Phil. in economic and social history from Oxford. Jessamine's essays have appeared most recently in *Hunger Mountain* and an anthology from Creative Nonfiction. She was also a three-night champion on Jeopardy! in 2012.

Cathy Porter

Infidels

even the warm winds
of summer can't salvage
this memory --

when we would talk
all night, never run out
of words

find new ones
to call out the prophets

who locked us
in blind faith

prayers tossed
to Saturday night infidels,
the ones doing everything

in full view of streetlights

where the bugs circle underneath,

on the lookout

for exposed skin –

a couple of worn faces

all out of beer and change

passing the hat

to anyone keeping score

from above

Cathy Porter's poetry has appeared in *Plainsongs, Chaffin Journal, Homestead Review, Kentucky Review, California Quarterly, Green Hills Literary Lantern, Hubbub,* and various other journals. She has two chapbooks available from *Finishing Line Press.* "A Life In The Day" (2012), and "Dust And Angels" (2014). Her latest chapbook, "Exit Songs," was published in 2016 from *Dancing Girl Press.* Cathy is a two-time Pushcart Prize nominee, and serves as a special editor for the journal *Fine Lines* in Omaha, NE.

T. E. Wilderson

Mother's Day

A toddler with a dozen plastic barrettes clipped in her matted hair was crawling around, wailing like a strangled cat on the scuffed linoleum floor in front of the Ray of Sunshine Homeless Shelter's lobby check-in desk. That morning, there was a ragtag group of loudly clacking people hanging about. All but an older white-haired woman wearing a badly pilled yellow crochet poncho quietly seated on the bulky beige sofa next to the stairwell were indifferent to the tense scene unfolding between a young couple near the entryway. The young woman's eyes were damp and red-rimmed, and her slack posture smacked of defeat.

"Dylan, don't go," said the young woman. She swiped her tear-soaked cheeks with the back of one bony hand, which she then dried on the hem of her holey pink T-shirt. Old marks from where she'd found escape in the prick of a needle heavily peppered her rail-thin arms.

"I gotta go," Dylan replied. "She's my mother." His attention was split between the young woman, April, and his yowling daughter.

"You don't gotta. What about me? I'm your baby's mother. Remember that?" April put her hands on her narrow hips and sniffled.

"I'll be back in a coupla hours. I already told you. We'll party when I get back." He seemed only vaguely sincere.

"Party? Party how?" April challenged.

"I dunno. We'll do something. It's early. Why don't you take Jasmine to the park?"

"It's fricking freezing out."

"So wear a jacket. Christ, do I have to think of everything?" He shoved past April and pushed open the wide glass doors.

April followed behind him and held the door ajar as she watched Dylan tromp down the steps and zip up his fleece jacket. The loose fabric of the sleeves flapped backward in the wind. She remained in the chilly doorway, watching, until he'd disappeared down the street. When she turned around and closed the door, she noticed the old poncho lady staring at her.

"The hell you looking at?" April asked.

~~~

Dylan was on the #7 bus that was slowly making its way through the downtown stretch of its route. He had his head leaned against the window and was gazing out. The bus passed an open florist. It was Sunday, and they were the only place doing business on an otherwise shut-down block. He pulled the signal cord and got off at the next stop. He had to double back a block and a half past a bank, a smoke shop, a Starbucks, and a FedEx to get to the floral shop. He also had to pass Shinder's bookstore—which mainly sold comic books and girlie magazines—and is where he'd amassed his precious *X-Men* collection, buying up editions of the comic when he had the money, and filching them when he didn't. Which was often. He'd come by his sticky fingers honestly from his mother, who knew how to secrete packs of luncheon meat and loaves of Wonder Bread in her large patchwork leather purse with the stealth of Houdini.

Dylan stood outside of the florist, and peered in at arrangements of irises, lilies, tulips, and bird-of-paradises through the plate glass window. He reached into the pocket of his scrubby jeans and pulled out a clump of cash. A number of coins fell to the ground as he uncrumpled the bills. He cursed under his breath as he chased a dime that was rolling away, picked up the other change, and counted what he had. Twelve dollars and sixty-two cents. He went inside.

"We're out of roses," said the taut-faced woman fashioning an elaborate bouquet behind the counter. She looked up and smiled tepidly at Dylan.

"That's okay," Dylan said. "I don't think I have rose money anyway."

The woman finished putting sprigs of baby's breath in the vase on the counter in front of her and met Dylan where he stood just inside the entryway. She gave him a cool once-over. "What are you looking for?" she asked.

Dylan laughed to himself. "What can I get for twelve dollars?"

~~~

Dylan was standing in front of a broke down, sooty, mint-colored duplex with torn shades in the bottom windows in the part of town considered the wrong side of the tracks. He was holding a bunch of eight cellophane-wrapped daisies, waiting for some sort of sign—exactly what he did not know—to propel him forward. It was May, but this was Minnesota, and he bristled at the crispy wind blowing about and cutting through his lightweight garments. His fingers were stiff and blanched from the cold. He slipped his cell phone out of his faded jeans pocket and checked the time: eleven forty-four. Tapping his finger on the weather icon revealed that it was fifty-one degrees—below average for that time of year to be sure and did not account for the wind chill. He put the phone back in his pocket, took in a deep breath, then went and rang the doorbell on the duplex's lower unit. The dingy door's white paint was peeling in flaky tendrils, and the dry-rot wood was cracked in spots. He waited. When no one answered he pounded hard, then stepped back and to the side as if he were halfway expecting buckshot to come spraying through the door at any moment. Dylan was turning to leave when he heard the door creak open. A fragile middle-aged woman appeared in the open sliver. She had mussed dark brunette hair, wore a drab, threadbare terry cloth bathrobe, and was missing a tobacco-stained upper right incisor.

"Hey," said the woman. "What time is it?" She had clearly been asleep. Pillow marks creased her puffy, sallow face.

"Hey, Mama," said Dylan. "Happy Mother's Day." He held the flowers out to her, but she just stared at them.

"Aw, hell. Thanks. You wanna come inside?"

"Nah, I gotta get back."

Dylan's mother, Crystal, let out a phlegmy laugh, and opened the door wider. "C'mon," she said. "Get your narrow ass in here—it's cold."

Dylan stepped inside the squalid home, and it took his eyes a moment to adjust to the dimness. The air was skunky with the smell of cigarettes, beer, and a whiff of dead rodent. He handed his mother the bouquet again. This time she took the daisies.

"I can't believe it. Flowers from my boy on Mother's Day. Lemme go get something to put them in." She shuffled off into the kitchen.

Dylan looked around for a clear place to sit. Finding none, he shoved some of the clothes piled on the sofa aside and sat down. He dolefully surveyed the familiar junky surroundings. The place was as oppressive as always, just as it had been when he had moved out shortly after his seventeenth birthday. It made him feel anxious and hemmed in, and in want of a long shower. His mother returned with a blue Tupperware pitcher.

"I guess this'll have to do," she said. She put the whole cellophane-wrapped bunch in the dry pitcher, then set it on top of the enormous cabinet television set, which was tuned to a pre-game football show. "Hey. Can I get you a beer?"

"No, Mama. I'm clean now, remember? Besides, it's not even noon."

"I'm clean now," she mimicked. "Look at me—I'm Mr. Clean. What's a *beer* gonna hurt? And it ain't noon yet? I didn't miss kickoff?"

"I don't think so. And I'll skip the beer, thanks. I'm this close to getting my one-year chip." He gestured with his fingers, pinching them about an inch apart. "It's going on ten-and-a-half months I've been clean and sober now."

"Hmmph. Again? How many times this make? I guess it's been a while since I seen you. You still with that skinny girl? She clean and sober too, I guess."

"April, Mama. You know her name. April. And yes, we kicked together."

His mother sat on top of some unopened mail, old magazines, and tattered chenille throw gathered on a tan pleather recliner that faced the television, and her eyes slipped shut for a split second. She caught herself about to fall asleep, then straightened herself in her seat.

"How's that little girl of yours? My grandbaby. Jasmine, ain't it?" she asked.

A corner of Dylan's mouth curled into a smile. "She's good. Real good." He laughed nervously.

"What's so funny?"

"Nothing," he shrugged.

"Y'all still living over in the projects?"

"Nah, we got put out. After I lost my job. Well, laid off. Downsized they called it. And April, you know, has to take care of Jasmine, so she can't work."

"The hell she can't. That's what daycare is for."

"I didn't come to fuss with you." Dylan's head drooped, and he kicked at the clutter by his feet.

"I'm sorry. I'm glad you came. My boy. Remembering his old mama on Mother's Day."

"I wanted to show you how good I been doing. I even got a job interview on Tuesday."

Crystal slapped her thigh. "Well good on you," she said. "What they gonna have you doing?"

"Sorting mail at this health clinic. Hopefully. If I get this job, I can get a place for me and April and Jasmine."

"Where you say you living now?"

Dylan shifted in his seat as he spoke. "For the time being we're staying in a shelter. But it's a good one. One that takes families, and they don't, you know, separate us like in most places. We're all together. It was hard getting in there. There's a waiting list. We waited over two months to get a spot." He glanced at his mother for approval, but all that he found was insouciance in her half-closed eyes. She crossed then uncrossed her legs, and there was a stiff silence buffered only by the chatter of the television sportscasters. She crossed her legs again, and began to wriggle the shabby, fuzzy house slipper dangling on the tips of her right toes. On the television, the kickoff was announced. Crystal glanced too late to catch it. She turned her focus back to her son.

"Say, how about we go by Liquor Lyle's so I can show everybody my flowers?"

He shook his head. "I don't think that's a good idea."

"Aw, c'mon. You don't gotta drink. Have a Pepsi or something. I just wanna show you off."

Dylan leaned his elbows on his knees, placed his head in his hands, and closed his eyes to avoid his mother's gaze.

"Just for a little bit," Crystal said. "You came all the way over here. Watch, I'm gonna get dressed, then we'll go."

Dylan sighed, then leaned back into the sofa, and folded his arms across his chest. "Can I bum a smoke?"

"Sure. There's a pack on the coffee table. Somewhere. I'ma go get dressed."

He rummaged through empty beer bottles, dirty dishes, and fast food wrappers until he found a pack of Newports and an ashtray with a dead fly in it. He tapped a cigarette from the box, pulled a silver Zippo from his jacket pocket, and lit the cigarette. No sooner had he taken in his second deep puff than his mother reappeared wearing a lavender velour jogging suit with dirty cuffs and a splotchy stain on one leg.

"C'mon," she said. "Let's go."

"You ain't gonna comb your hair or nothing?"

"Nah, they know me there." She shrugged on her tan corduroy jacket, then raked her hands through her messy mane. "Let's go."

They left the house, and she locked the door behind them. Halfway down the walk his mother stopped and said, "Wait! Let's go show Old Gladys upstairs what you brung me."

"Why? I thought you didn't like her."

"I don't, but I bet she ain't got no flowers today. And, she's always looking at me like I ain't shit." They went back up the walk. Crystal rang her neighbor's doorbell, then impatiently rapped on the door. She bounced on her heels as they waited. "Shit. It's cold, ain't it?" she said.

Dylan nodded. "You know, we'll stay a minute, then I really gotta go."

"That's crazy talk. Don't let that little heifer run you 'round."

Dylan was about to speak when the upstairs neighbor's jowly round face peered briefly at them through the small, paned window above the broken-hinged knocker. Recognizing Crystal, she opened the door. She was dressed in a navy-blue, boiled-wool suit with a garnet brooch pinned to the lapel, and thick ivory hose. Her feet bubbled out of wide patent leather pumps with gold buckles across the instep.

"Hey, how you do?" Gladys said. She regarded the duo on her doorstep cautiously, as if they might turn out to be selling vacuums.

"I'm doing great," Crystal said. "You remember my boy, Dylan."

"Sure, sure."

"We just came by to say 'Happy Mother's Day.'"

"Oh. Thank you." She made no move to open the door any wider.

"He brung me these." Crystal shoved the flowers so close to Gladys's face it caused the old woman to lean back a bit. "Ain't you gonna invite us in?"

Gladys, taken off guard, opened the door and asked them inside. Once she'd hobbled upstairs with mother and son trailing behind her, she told them to make themselves at home in the pristine living room. Dylan sat close to his mother on the plastic-covered, olive-green damask sofa. The older woman sat across from them on the edge of a matching plastic-covered armchair, her hands folded in her lap. Crystal cradled her bouquet of daisies like a baby. No one spoke for a good minute, and they just exchanged uneasy glances at each other. The only perceptible noises were the ticking of a sunburst wall clock, and the low strains of gospel music coming from a radio in the kitchen toward the back of the house.

"So. I guess you went to church this morning," Crystal finally said.

"I go to church every morning," Gladys responded tersely.

"You shitting me. Every morning?"

"Always have."

"Hmmph. That's something. I ain't been to church since I don't know when."

"There's something to be said for keeping the Lord in your life."

"The Lord gave up on me years ago," Crystal cackled. "But he's looking out for my boy, ain't he? He got a interview coming up for a good job. A real good job." She nodded at her son. "Don't you, Dylan?"

Dylan forced a timorous smile and nodded.

"And, he's living uptown now. He and his family. He's got a little girl, you know. She's how old?"

"She'll be three next month," Dylan said meekly. He couldn't bring himself to correct her about where he lived.

"You got any pictures of her? Show us some pictures. You got any on your phone?"

Dylan fished his cell phone out of his pocket and pulled up a shot of his daughter holding a Mylar balloon next to a Chucky Cheese figure.

"Lemme see." Crystal took the phone from her son and squinted at the screen. "She ain't got no teeth yet?"

"Well, she lost her front teeth." He fidgeted with his fingers. "They say it's because we let her sleep with a juice bottle at night... Not that she was born addicted to, you know, the methadone or anything. She's got a few teeth in the back she chews with."

"Well, at least they're baby teeth. I guess. Her grown-up teeth'll come in, won't they?"

"They say they will."

"I hope so. Go show her."

Dylan took the phone from his mother and brought it over to Gladys so that she could take a look. The old woman glimpsed first at the phone, then at Dylan.

"She's cute," Gladys said unctuously. "Real cute."

Dylan thanked her, then returned to his seat next to his mother, who took the phone from him.

"She looks a lot like you," Crystal said. "Especially them eyes. And 'round about the nose. Mmm hmm."

"Most people think she looks like April," Dylan said.

Crystal scrunched up her face, then handed back his phone. She looked at Gladys. "You got plans for Mother's Day?"

"As a matter of fact, my niece is on her way to pick me up for brunch. We're going to the buffet out at the casino."

"Well, good on you," Crystal said. Insincerity coated her voice. She scratched at her scalp. "We got plans too, don't we, Dylan? As a matter of fact, we oughta be going. C'mon Dylan."

Crystal stood, and Dylan followed her lead.

Gladys rose to see them out, relief washing over her face.

"Being so holy and all, I don't see you as the gambling type," Crystal called to Gladys over her shoulder.

"I'm not, but they've got a special brunch today, and I love a good buffet," Gladys replied. She lumbered slowly down the stairs behind them to the door, her grasp firm on the handrail.

"Happy Mother's Day," Dylan timidly said to Gladys as she swiftly closed the door behind him and his mother.

~~~

Liquor Lyle's never closed. To call it a dive would be generous, with its worn high-backed red Naugahyde booths lining the back wall, tall tables along the front, and horseshoe-shaped bar commanding the center of the room. The concrete floor was sticky. Neon signs promoting Coors, Rolling Rock, Miller Lite, Pabst, Schlitz, and Budweiser provided most of the light in the dank place, along with what little was filtering in from the yellow plastic transom window. There were a half-dozen denizens hunched over their drinks. A few of them looked up when the shock of daylight burst in the place when Dylan and his mother stepped inside. They took seats at the bar, and were greeted warmly by Aaron, the bartender.

"This here's my boy," Crystal said with a broad smile. She caught the eye of one of the other patrons. "You hear that, Billy? Don't think I don't see you down there."

A slovenly man in a brown leather bomber jacket down the bar raised his glass and nodded at Dylan and his mother.

"Yeah, you know it's Mother's Day, and my boy brung me these here." She waved the bouquet of daisies in the air for all to see. "Get him a drink, will you, Aaron." She turned to Dylan. "What are you having?"

"I'll have a ginger ale," Dylan said to the bartender.

"That's it? We're celebrating. Live a little. Gimme some Southern Comfort—and make it a double. Hey, you know who drank Southern

Comfort? Janis Joplin. Drank it day and night. Southern Comfort—it's not just for breakfast anymore." She hacked a bit and thumped her chest a couple of times with her fist. "We still can't smoke in here?"

The bartender shook his head.

"Fine," said Crystal. "Hey, put a little Jack in that ginger ale!"

"No, Mama," said Dylan. He wagged his finger at the bartender. "Forget the Jack, just the ginger ale."

"Since when did you become such a killjoy? What's one drink gonna do?"

"Nothing good. I'm doing my best to stay straight, Mama. I don't want my girls to have to stay in a shelter. I gotta stay straight, get this job, then get us outta there. Besides, we can't stay in shelters and halfway houses forever. Getting split up and all that half the time. It's no way I want my baby to have to grow up. Living on the street . . ."

"Yeah, well," Crystal said. "We made it on the street when we had to. Didn't we? Or is Miss April too good for that kind of living?"

"Nobody should have to live on the street. Ever. I gotta take care of my girls." He looked at his mother with disbelief tinged with dismay.

"I'm just saying *we* made it is all. It's not like we were always totally homeless. We had a car to live in for a while. Remember that?"

"No. I don't remember."

"Well, we did. And you don't know what I had to do to *get* that car." She soughed to herself. Dylan didn't need to be reminded of the steady stream of men that used to come through the house—when they had a house—clearing their throats and buckling their belts on their way out the door. He'd been invisible to them, as he sat on the floor playing his Nintendo, heeding stern instructions not to disturb Mama while she was "entertaining."

Aaron came with Crystal's Southern Comfort, and a tall glass of ginger ale with a sidecar of Jack Daniels for Dylan. Crystal loudly slapped the bar when she saw the whiskey.

"Now that's what I'm talking about! Thanks, handsome!" She gave the bartender the thumbs up as he headed down to the other end toward Billy.

"Happy Mother's Day," Aaron called back.

"Now we're in business! How you like me now!" she hooted. She swung her daisies in a circle above her head.

Dylan stared at the glass of liquor for the length of the car commercial playing on the muted television hanging in the far corner of the bar. He ran his finger in circles around the rim of the tumbler of whiskey, while absently dunking the thin red straw in and out of the ginger ale. He focused on the sound of the ice cubes knocking around in the tall glass.

"C'mon," said Crystal. "Let's toast. To mother-effing Mother's Day!" She raised her glass and looked eagerly at her son.

Dylan dropped his head. He paused for a long moment and stared at the two drinks in front of him. His shoulders shuddered as he let out a quiet, sardonic laugh. "Nah, I really can't," he finally said.

"Seriously? You won't toast your old mama? After all we been through?"

"I'll toast you with my ginger ale." He picked up the tall glass.

"Forget it. It ain't the same."

"C'mon Mama . . ."

"No. That's alright. I got but one boy, and all I'm asking is he share a toast with me. On Mother's Day." She sat with one elbow leaning on the bar, her glass poised in the air, and regarded her son through narrowed eyes. A slight smirk smudged her face.

Dylan heaved a huge sigh, then picked up the whiskey and clinked glasses with Crystal. "To Mother's Day," he said.

~~~

The day had faded into the starchy darkness of a chilled spring night.

Jasmine was sprawled out, flailing and wailing, in dirty footy pajamas on the floor of the homeless shelter's lobby.

"But he's only ten minutes late!" April shouted at Nate, the counselor who had the misfortune of manning the check-in desk that night. He had the build of a heavyweight boxer, slicked-back black hair, and the unflappable air of a Buckingham Palace guard.

"Rules are rules—you know that," Nate replied calmly. He looked at Dylan collapsed outside in a heap against the glass doors. "And more than being late, he's drunk. You know the rules."

"Screw your rules!" spat April. "Come on Jas, get up." She reached down, grabbed the toddler's hand, and dragged the child kicking and screaming toward the locked lobby doors. When the little girl saw that it was her father outside, she stood up and began slapping her small hands on the glass.

"Dada!" Jasmine cried but went unacknowledged.

"I just called my mom," Dylan gurgled, as he fumbled to put away his phone. "She said she's still at Liquor Lyle's and meet her there."

"Don't do that! Baby, just don't. Go find a shelter. Go to St. Matthew's. Or Crossroads. Then come back tomorrow," April said.

"She said I can crash at her house. It's just for tonight. I swear it." He leaned his back to the doors, and sat legs splayed, facing the street.

April furiously banged her fists on the glass. "Go *anywhere* but your mom's!"

Dylan grappled his way up to leave. April cursed riotously at Dylan, then railed against his mother: What kind of mother was she? What had she done to him? What had he done to *them*? She turned around and looked at Nate, exasperated and desperate, tears coursing freely down her face. When the man just shook his head at her, she spun back to face Dylan, who stumbled as he turned to go.

Jasmine grabbed onto her mother's leg. She threw her head back, her crying jagged and delirious.

"Dylan, please," April plead. "Please . . ."

The young drunk scrubbed his hand over his face, then careened sideways down the steps to the sidewalk.

Dylan paused, wavering unsteadily, as if to get his bearings. Then he shoved his hand into the right back pocket of his jeans and pulled out a crimped bus pass.

If only he were to look back, he'd see April and Jasmine pressed against the Ray of Sunshine's glass doors, hoping. Hoping.

Instead, he lurched forward into the wind a few steps, then stopped.

T. E. Wilderson is a Midwestern writer who also works as a graphic designer and copywriter. Wilderson's work has appeared in *Crack the Spine*, *the Roanoke Review*, *The Louisville Review*, and is forthcoming in the *Notre Dame Review*. A graduate of Spalding University's MFA writing program, Wilderson is at work on a short story collection and a novel.

Christina Wiseman

Route 2

Rushes of white light came at the girls as cars streaked by underneath them. They felt the wind on their legs, tanned and dangling through the overpass rails like the bendy straws in their Cokes. Annie's flip-flop had slipped off once and the two of them had shrieked with laughter and horror watching it fall onto the highway below.

On these summer nights the damp air coated their bodies and coaxed out their goosebumps. They ached with dangerous wonder (hormones). The lights kept coming.

They screamed to know what it felt like, guttural and deep and loud as they could.

Christina Wiseman has completed the Novel Generator program, a competitive-entry intensive workshop at Boston's *GrubStreet* creative writing center. She lives in Somerville, Massachusetts and is currently at work on her first novel.

Mariah Perkins

Miss

I catch gender in my teeth
like softballs:
jaw-breaking, bloodied mouth
until everything tastes like pennies.

Slouched shoulders of not wearing a bra,
blood stained bed sheets,
hairs pulling on tights—
forgetting to pay the female tax.
I have a bad taste in my mouth

there is so much blood in here—
I start spitting
leaving cherry stains on freshly published books.
I start choking
on the iron of teeth cracking.
I start revisiting
the softball thrown at my ten year old mouth.

It tasted new

like first kiss lip biting—

okay, at first,

not knowing what to do with my hands

discovering that I had no need for them

except to apply make-up over the bruised jaw.

I felt my bones re-growing

forming hips to signify womb almost ready,

growing pains shooting from toe to shoulder

making my walk look more like a dance,

I became a parade—

or participation trophy

forced into a display case.

I wanted to grow down

or inward

revisiting my own blood,

it looks the same

as the iron found leaking in my mouth—

but it began to seem less like a game.

Mariah Perkins is a poet from Grand Rapids, MI. She is currently an MFA candidate at Wichita State University. She was a winner of the *Mentally Distilled Poetry Slam* and you can find interviews with her in *SkipFiction* (Grand Rapids Culture Blog) and WYCE's *Electric Poetry*.

Devon Balwit

Stargazing on Easter Island

We are all waiting to go home, promises made, but not kept. We face the firmament, the hollows of our eye sockets especially wistful. Heat lightning slices a bright jag. If we had legs, we would dash its bridge. Instead, to outsiders, we look ridiculous, like a line of plebes, stiff before a breezeless flag, chins jutting to cover our embarrassment.

Devon Balwit writes in Portland, OR. She has five chapbooks out or forthcoming: "How the Blessed Travel" (*Maverick Duck Press*); "Forms Most Marvelous" (*dancing girl press*); "In Front of the Elements" *(Grey Borders Books)*, "Where You Were Going Never Was" (*Grey Borders Books*); and "The Bow Must Bear the Brunt" (*Red Flag Poetry*). Her individual poems can be found in *The Cincinnati Review, The Stillwater Review, Red Earth Review, The Fourth River; The Ekphrastic Review; Anti-Heroin Chic, The Inflectionist; Muse A/Journal*, and more.

Christina Kapp

Waste Removal

Lauren, who had a tendency to pass out on the couch at 10:00pm, left her cherry pits, sucked clean and coupled with their amputated stems, on the coffee table in the bottom of an empty water glass.

Marty, who had nocturnal tendencies and could never find anything worth watching on TV, took Lauren's glass and put it in the sink. This was less an effort to rein in the debris around their apartment than to give a purpose to his pacing, which had more to do with Lauren's misplaced body than her discarded cherry pits. As he made his circuit through the four small but distinct spaces in the apartment—living room, bedroom, bathroom, kitchen—he found several other things to banish to the sink as well: two plates with red splotches of pizza, a soda cup with a plastic lid and straw, a coffee cup half full of light, congealing liquid, and an empty ice cream container with a spoon.

"What the fuck is this shit?" he said out loud, knowing perfectly well what each item was and exactly how it had come to be in its place.

Marty and Lauren had lived together for a year, so Marty knew that unlike many of the other abandoned items lying around the apartment, the zigzag shape that was Lauren's person would require a conversation to move, one which he wasn't inclined to have. Therefore, when he grew tired of moving the non-verbal items around, he went to bed alone.

In the morning, Lauren got up and made a pot of coffee. She poured a bowl of cereal and ate it. She left the empty box of cereal and the bowl on the kitchen counter and poured the coffee into a mug. She poured some creamer into the coffee and left the container and the spoon on the counter as well. Then she took the mug with her into the bathroom.

Marty, shedding the blurriness of morning, wandered into the kitchen.

"For Christ's sake!" he exclaimed, even though he knew that Christ had not been in his apartment eating breakfast.

He went back to the bedroom where the drawers hung open. He stood there for a moment, then he went back to the kitchen where the bowl and spoon yawned at him. Then he went back to the bedroom where the pillows sprawled on the floor. Then he went back to the kitchen where drips of coffee stared at him from the counter. Then he went back to the bedroom where Lauren's pajama bottoms curled up on the bed. Each time he stopped moving, he became more and more irate about the morning's remains lying out in the open. However, Marty's pacing still wasn't about the cleanliness of the apartment, or at least that wasn't the primary reason. This time Marty paced because he had to pee, and he knew that Lauren's bathroom habits could waste an hour like a souvenir shopper in Times Square trying to decide between the Statue of Liberty figurine and the Empire State Building paperweight. Given this, he felt he had no choice but to take matters into his own hands, so to speak.

His presence at the toilet caused Lauren to stick her wet, semi-soapy head out from behind the shower curtain.

"Can't you give me five minutes of privacy?" she yelled at him.

As he finished peeing, he noticed her cup of coffee sitting on the counter, exactly where yesterday's cup had been when he picked it up the night before. The creamer was already thickening around the rim. There was a towel on the floor and an empty bottle of Aveeno Active Naturals Body Wash lying sideways in the sink.

"How can there be a towel on the floor?" he asked through the shower curtain. "You're not even out of the shower yet."

Lauren stuck her hand out from behind the curtain and shooed him away. Marty went back to the kitchen and put the dishes in the dishwasher, which was starting to smell like a dead thing. He put in the detergent and turned it on. He put the empty cereal box into the recycling and the plastic liner into the garbage, but the can was full, so he pulled the top of the bag over the trash and leaned into it, making room for a little bit more.

Marty did these things not because he had OCD, a neat streak, or any discernable aesthetic sense at all, but because he had come to feel as though world around him had simply stopped moving forward. Everything was stuck in all the wrong places. He wasn't one to waste time on philosophical musings, but if he had tried to describe the feeling, he might have said that it was as though God was a giant juggler who had become bored with the trick of keeping the planets and the things on them in motion, and simply let the universe hit the ground in whatever haphazard order it fell. Somehow, by Marty's thinking, it was up to people, and him in particular, to get rid of the extraneous stuff and put everything back in motion again.

"What is your problem this morning?" Lauren had turned off the shower and was yelling at him from inside the bathroom.

Marty turned on the garbage disposal to drown out her question, causing an unexpected clatter and screech which shut down the motor altogether. Lauren appeared in the kitchen doorway wearing a towel. Her hair was dripping down her shoulders and water was pooling at her feet.

"Seriously, Marty. What are you doing?"

Marty leaned over the sink and flipped the disposal switch up and down. He did this not because he thought it was going to come back on—he knew he had killed it—but because it occurred to him that putting the morning back into its proper motion might take more skill and self-control than he currently possessed.

"Serves you right," Lauren said. Her tone implied a crossing of arms and an "I told you so" that wasn't necessary, but of course she said it anyway. "I told you we shouldn't have a one of those. They're not allowed."

"Yes, they are," Marty said, exhaling with each word. Part of him wanted to grab Lauren by the naked shoulders and walk her and her towel out the front door so he could get ready for work in peace, but instead he corrected her: "Garbage disposals have not been illegal in New York City buildings since 1997. Plus, I got permission."

"I didn't say they were illegal, I said they're not allowed. No one else in this building has one. You told the super you were putting in a new sink, not a garbage grinder."

He wanted to tell her these things: 1) "Grinder" was not the correct word for this particular device, 2) a garbage disposal was a very efficient way to get rid of food waste, and 3) the super didn't have anything to say about it. But there was no point. Having this conversation was a waste of precious pre-work minutes, and while the towel and her drippiness did suggest a certain opportunity, it was safe to assume that her near-naked presence wasn't the come-on he would have liked it to be. Those moments were among the few things he did not tend to find scattered around the apartment.

As if reading his mind, Lauren deftly rewrapped the towel more snugly around herself without yielding even a momentary flash of skin. When she walked away, Marty wiped up the spot where she had stood and went to take a shower.

~~~

Marty and Lauren worked in adjacent buildings near Columbus Circle. That was how they had met. They were both eating lunch in the park. And this morning, as Marty sat in a meeting whose agenda seemed solely to consist of scheduling more meetings, the park seemed an appropriate place to end the relationship. It wasn't, he determined, that he didn't find her attractive, or even that he didn't like her. It was more that her presence had multiplied. She was everywhere, even when she wasn't there. Whatever relationship efficiencies might have been gained by having her in close proximity were then lost by having so much more of her to navigate around.

In any case, there was a certain symmetry to ending it in the park. He was even thinking that it would be nice to sit on the same bench.

"It's been a good ride," he would say. "But we just aren't going anywhere. We're stuck. In a rut."

When he returned to his office after the meeting, there were three very long texts from Lauren about what to eat for lunch. To save time, Marty typed "same spot," and went back to work, presuming that whatever additional issues had come up could be dealt with when he saw her. There was no reason to get into them now.

At lunch, he met Lauren at the entrance to the park. It was a warm, bright day and the streets were crowded. Lauren wanted a croque-monsieur from the bistro kiosk, but the line was long and Marty was getting hot just standing around.

"You can make a grilled cheese anytime you want," he said.

"But these are really good. What do you want?" Lauren asked.

"I want to get out of here."

"If you don't like the croque-monsieur, they have other things, too."

"It's fine," Marty replied, watching the pigeons peck at the ground. He stomped at one of them and watched it fly away. "Can't you just get something else? There's a hot dog cart right over there."

"It will just take a minute. Anyway, you can share mine. I never finish the whole thing."

When Lauren had her sandwich, they walked down the path into the park. It was quieter off the main walkways and Marty sped up, trying to stretch his legs, but Lauren protested, citing her less than comfortable shoes and the beautiful day.

"What's your rush?" she asked.

As they approached their usual bench, the bench that Marty had imagined for the occasion, he noticed that the garbage can next to it was overflowing with something dark. Whatever it was stuck up farther than items usually did out of garbage cans, and his first thought was that it was a bundle of roof shingles or some other construction material, but that didn't make sense.

He stopped, unable to figure it out.

Lauren sat on the bench next to the garbage can. She removed the sandwich from the paper bag in her lap and opened a plastic bottle of water. She took a sip and held it out to Marty.

Marty moved slowly toward the garbage can. What stuck out of the top was, quite distinctly, the nose of an animal. The poor creature's black mass sprouted through the mesh holes of the can in a bristly diamond pattern. On the bench, Lauren waved away a fly and took a bite of her sandwich.

"Come on, sit down," Lauren said, and when Marty didn't respond, her voice turned to a growl. "What's your problem?"

"Get up."

"What?"

He reached forward and jerked her off the bench, causing her sandwich to slip off her lap and land on the ground with a small, fleshy slap.

"Hey!" she said, pulling away.

"Don't you see? Don't you pay any attention to anything at all?" Marty felt the blood swelling in his veins like a balloon overfilled with air to the point of bursting.

"Yes, I pay attention. I pay attention to you wrecking my lunch. What's wrong with you?"

"There's a dog in that garbage can."

She turned around and, for a moment, both of them were silent. The dog was large and seemed to have been dumped lengthwise into the can with his face and two paws sticking out the top. He couldn't have been dead for very long. The dog's eye was open but flat, like a dark fingernail. His mouth hung open in a way that insinuated a very human call for help and showed a ridge of yellowed teeth nestled into gums that had gone grey. Two flies rose from the tip of the dog's nose and returned to it again.

Lauren put her hand over her mouth and whispered, "poor thing." Then she turned and started to walk away.

"Where are you going?" Marty said, reaching out and grabbing her wrist.

"Anywhere but here. It could have some kind of disease. Let's go over by the playground. They have food carts there." She paused, then said, "Looks like you're going to get your hot dog after all."

Marty held her wrist tightly and stared at her. Lauren was all straight lines—long nose, long hair, sharp chin—but he could swear that he had seen the curve of a smile on her face when she said the words "hot dog." He could feel the pull of her body, leaning away and drawing him with her, as if this massive dead thing left out in the open for all to see was nothing more than a pizza box or a plastic bag to be sidestepped and ignored.

"Lauren, don't you have a heart?"

He said this before he had a chance to think about it and later these would be the words he couldn't stop hearing in his head, but as they stood there, the sense that she was dead inside was overwhelming and infuriating. Then, to make matters worse, she laughed, and although it was just a little laugh, and really just the sort of laugh that people do when they see something awkward or uncomfortable, it spurred Marty into a sort of rage. Lauren crouched and braced herself as Marty tried to drag her back to the trash can and the dead dog. She screeched like furniture being pulled across a floor but refused to move. He heard himself saying things like, "you just can't just do things like this," and "there are more important things in this world than you" and he felt his grip tighten when she tried to pull away. She was yelling his name, telling him to stop, but it all felt irrelevant, detached from the seconds ticking by on his watch or the breaths plunging in and out of his lungs.

The police officer came from behind and was nearly within arm's reach before Marty saw him.

"Sir, let go of her," the officer said. His voice was hard and dark, like a metal post.

Marty released his grip.

"Is everything alright here, ma'am?"

"There's a dog in the trash can," Marty said.

The officer stepped between Marty and Lauren and repeated his question to Lauren.

"Do you know this man?" he asked her.

Lauren didn't respond. She just stood there rubbing her wrist and looking at Marty as if the answer to the question was not at all clear.

"Excuse me, but there is a dead dog," Marty said again, louder this time.

The officer continued to ignore him. Marty walked a few steps toward the dog, then back again to where Lauren was explaining that she and Marty were in the park having lunch. The officer asked to see Lauren's wrist and she showed it to him, which Marty didn't want to see, so he walked back toward the dog again, then, on realizing that the officer still hadn't bothered to turn his head to see the fur, the snout, and the dead eye that was staring at all of them, he turned and came back to Lauren and the officer.

Marty told himself he was pacing not because he didn't know that people were cruel, but because he was giving the officer time to come to his senses, and see what needed to be seen, but when the officer looked like he was about to go without even addressing the true problem in this scenario, he addressed the officer more forcefully, rushing back toward the two of them and inserting himself between Lauren and the officer in order to make his point. However, in doing so he accidentally stepped on Lauren's foot. She screamed—

unnecessarily dramatically, he thought—and pushed Marty forward, which caused him to topple into the officer who now standing directly in front of him.

The force of Marty's body hitting the officer's chest was certainly not something he intended, but Lauren was stronger than she looked. More regretfully, he felt himself put a forearm—and elbow—out to protect himself, which, unfortunately, struck the shorter police officer in the chin.

From that point Marty was not entirely clear—and he would rather not speculate—whether he fell to the ground on his own or the officer had in some manner put him there, but he was acutely aware that a pain resembling a minor sun had taken up residence in the back of his skull. Above him, Lauren's protests smacked the air like the wings of pigeons taking flight. A second officer appeared between Marty's face and the sky. The two cops pulled him to his feet. For the next thirty seconds or so, it felt like there were more hands on his body than he could account for as they turned him to face the fence lining the path, ordered him to put his hands on it, and patted him down. Spit gathered in his mouth and he sucked it in and choked. He coughed uncontrollably for a minute or two. Then, as he was trying to get his lips and tongue to arrange themselves into something approximating an explanation, the first officer asked, "Sir, is that your animal?"

Lauren made a snorting sound behind him. Marty turned his head to try to see the dog, and in doing so noted that a crowd had started to gather. People were taking pictures of him with their cell phones, visual tchotchkes of the Crazy Man to pass around among family, friends, and co-workers. He imagined them telling their dinner companions about him. Pictures of the Crazy Man would clutter their phones for days, months, and possibly years even as the dog was forgotten—if they had even noticed he was there. He heard Lauren giving the police his name, her name. She stumbled over a recitation of their address. The police officer asked if he needed medical assistance.

"No. I think I'm fine."

The officers went one way and Marty and Lauren went another, heading back up the path and out of the park. Lauren was silent as they passed the bistro kiosk and the still long lines for grilled cheese with a French surcharge. Marty knew she was angry. He knew he had behaved badly, and he struggled to rid himself of images he now carried in his head: the dead dog, the upside down croque-monsieur, the officers, the crowds, the look on Lauren's face as they left the park and joined the throngs of tourists on the sidewalk. He hadn't wanted any of these things.

He felt dizzy and disoriented. At the light at the corner they stopped and she looked at him, her face smooth and clean as an empty room. He wanted to see their bedroom, a shower full of shampoo bottles, and a sink full of dishes, but it was as though she had been scrubbed down to an outline, and he struggled to fill in the gaps.

"It was dead," he said.

She nodded and looked down Sixth Avenue, toward midtown, where they never went for lunch. "Yes," she replied and when the light changed, she walked off on her own, leaving Marty standing on the corner, hanging on to the sound of her voice drifting up into the air.

Christina Kapp's short fiction, poetry, and essays have appeared in numerous publications including *Limestone, Passages North, Barn Owl Review, Gargoyle, DOGZPLOT, Storyscape Journal, PANK, Anderbo.com*, and *apt*. She teaches at The Writers Circle Workshops in Summit, NJ.

Sarah Broussard Weaver

Turquoise & Tiger's Eye

When the time came, and I felt a needle pushing through my nostril, I examined the feeling closely. This allowed my mind to escape, helping me separate my fear of pain from the reality of the pressure—not quite pain but so near it as to allow panic. I longed to leap away and run. The sensation was clearly wrong, something a body shouldn't feel. My mind knew I had paid good money for this woman to shove a needle through my cartilage, but my muscles tried to move into survival mode. The slow pierce, a breaking and entering, seemed to last an hour, but my daughter's iPhone—used to video the event—later revealed it had not even been two minutes. What would we do without technology to tell us what really happened? I suppose I could claim to you an hour of pressure, or twenty minutes of pain, whatever my body interpreted as truth. You wouldn't believe me—would you?— but you would have no authority to argue. But a preteen's iPhone, wearing a plastic case bearing the motto "Faction before blood," has authority over my experience. I dare not demur.

Afterward, examining my body's newest hole in a turquoise hand-held mirror, I was surprised to realize that my main thoughts were of impermanence. If I removed the stud—a small yellow tiger's eye—immediately, after being in its place for only two minutes, would my nose look the same? Would it bear a mark? How long until the hole knit its sides back together? And if I wore my stud for a year, what then? How long did I have before my decision would mark me forever?

I stared at my nose in the mirror and wondered at the lack of blood. There had been one drop, wiped away quickly by my piercer. Was it the quickness of her needle or did my nose hold few blood vessels? Had the hole been neutralized, consoled, by being quickly met with a platinum stud to fill the loss of flesh?

There had been one blood-drop and one teardrop. I didn't cry, not really, but somehow a salty one-tear-trail had leaked from my clenched eyes as I dissected my feelings and she pushed the needle. Involuntary and embarrassing. I felt betrayed by my body. I told the woman, still holding a barely bloody tissue, that I didn't know why I'd cried, that I hadn't done it, that it had just happened. She said it was normal and told me not to worry. I felt like telling her I wasn't worried but wasn't sure if that was true. I wasn't sure why it seemed so important to appear unruffled and unhurt to this woman who makes her living by pushing needles through people's bodies. Surely she would not remember me, whether I cried or not. Unless my muscles had won and shoved me out of her chair, I'd fade away into a cozy blur, the newly pierced, the ruined or bettered bodies, the way she earns her daily bread.

Eventually I dealt with my thoughts of impermanence in my usual lazy way, by just ignoring them. What does it matter if a mark remains? My body is 39 years old, already the canvas of my life, bearing scars and freckles, moles and lines. I resolved to enjoy my new acquisition without thinking of its aftermath. I've already spent too much time in my life worrying about my choices and their consequences. Whatever comes with my body's new hole will be fine with me., By overcoming fears of what family and friends will think, by urging my muscles to ignore their response, by paying $75 and bringing my official state ID, by not ripping the eye of a tiger out after two minutes of staring in a turquoise mirror, I've earned the right to wear this jewel.

Sarah Broussard Weaver is currently working on her MFA in creative nonfiction at the Rainier Writing Workshop at Pacific Lutheran University. Her essays have been published in *Lunch Ticket, Hippocampus, The Nervous Breakdown, and Full Grown People,* among others.

www.ingramcontent.com/pod-product-compliance
Lightning Source LLC
Chambersburg PA
CBHW070551180626
46817CB00005B/1785